BRIEF GREEK SYNTAX

BRIEF GREEK SYNTAX

BY

LOUIS BEVIER, Jr., Ph.D.

PROFESSOR OF THE GREEK LANGUAGE AND LITERATURE
IN RUTGERS COLLEGE

College Classical Series
CARATZAS BROTHERS, PUBLISHERS
NEW ROCHELLE, NEW YORK

1981

Exact reprint of the original edition. Published by,

Caratzas Brothers, Publishers
481 Main Street (Box 210)
New Rochelle, New York 10802
U.S.A.

PREFACE

MANY experienced college teachers of Greek will agree in the opinion that the changes in preparatory school methods during the last decade or two have resulted in giving us freshmen whose knowledge of Greek syntax is vague and general rather than clear and precise. This may be traced to various causes. Grammar drill has been in part displaced by wider reading to meet the "sight-reading" tests in the college entrance examinations. The "natural method" has not been without its baleful influence. No doubt many minor causes have been at work; but, whatever the causes, the fact is beyond question. The average freshman of to-day has a vague and general knowledge of Greek syntax, instead of the clear and precise grasp of fundamental principles which he needs.

Now if the college course in Greek is to consist largely of the study of the masterpieces of Greek literature as literature, such clear and precise knowledge must, at some time, be acquired, or else real appreciation is out of the question. It is idle for even the bright student to read the great *Apology* and hope to appreciate it as literature, unless he knows something definite of the normal use of moods and tenses. Else he may admire with enthusiasm what he takes to be the force and beauty of the Greek language, or the precision and flexibility of the author's style, but quite as likely as not he is applauding in the wrong place.

A reaction, emphasizing once more the importance of grammar in the preparatory study of Greek, is, I believe,

PREFACE

bound to come. The aim of this little book is to supply a means to further this result. In it I have briefly formulated the essentials of Greek syntax as simply and as clearly as I could. It is, of course, intended principally for use in preparatory schools, and will, it is hoped, economize the time of the student by directing attention to essentials, leaving details for later study. At the same time it is quite possible that such a summary may not come amiss to many freshmen for purposes of review. It need scarcely be said that it is not intended to take the place of the more extensive grammars already in use.

All statements of principle are illustrated by examples quoted in their actual form. Their arrangement has been designed to secure as much clearness as possible. For obvious reasons the quotations are drawn chiefly from the *Anabasis*. A few, however, come from Homer, and still fewer from the *Cyropaedia* and other writings of Xenophon, and from prose writers in general.

In preparing this book I have been under obligations to my colleague, Professor William Hamilton Kirk, and to the editor-in-chief of this series of text-books, Professor Herbert Weir Smyth of Harvard University, for many helpful criticisms and suggestions. To both these scholars I hereby extend my cordial thanks.

L. BEVIER, Jr.

RUTGERS COLLEGE,
NEW BRUNSWICK, N. J.

CONTENTS

SECTIONS		PAGE
1– 14.	THE CONCORDS	9
15– 30.	THE ARTICLE	12
31– 43.	THE PRONOUNS	16
44–105.	THE CASES OF THE NOUN	20
44– 47.	THE NOMINATIVE	20
48.	THE VOCATIVE	21
49– 61.	THE ACCUSATIVE	21
62– 88.	THE GENITIVE	24
89–105.	THE DATIVE	31
106–120.	THE VOICES OF THE VERB	36
121–158.	THE TENSES OF THE INDICATIVE	40
124–131.	THE PRESENT TENSE	41
132–136.	THE IMPERFECT TENSE	42
137–140.	THE PERFECT TENSE	44
141–143.	THE PLUPERFECT TENSE	45
144–150.	THE AORIST TENSE	45
151–155.	THE FUTURE TENSE	47
156–158.	THE FUTURE PERFECT TENSE	48
159–196.	THE TENSES OF THE OTHER MOODS	49
160–162.	THE TENSES OF THE SUBJUNCTIVE	49
163–165, 173–177.	THE TENSES OF THE OPTATIVE	50
166–168.	THE TENSES OF THE IMPERATIVE	50
169–171, 178–182.	THE TENSES OF THE INFINITIVE	51
183–196.	THE TENSES OF THE PARTICIPLE	54
197–287.	THE MOODS OF THE VERB	57
197–210.	THE INDICATIVE MOOD	57
211–222.	THE SUBJUNCTIVE MOOD	61
223–238.	THE OPTATIVE MOOD	64

CONTENTS

SECTIONS		PAGE
239–241.	THE IMPERATIVE MOOD	66
242–261.	THE INFINITIVE MOOD	69
262–287.	THE PARTICIPLE	75
288–291.	THE VERBAL IN -τέος	82
292–296.	THE SEQUENCE OF MOODS AND TENSES	83
297–310.	INDIRECT DISCOURSE	85
300–302.	INDIRECT QUESTIONS	86
311–325.	CONDITIONAL SENTENCES	89
326–333.	THE PARTICLE Ἄν	94
334–344.	THE NEGATIVE PARTICLES Οὐ AND Μή	96
345–358.	THE PREPOSITIONS	99
345–349.	PREPOSITIONS GOVERNING ONE CASE	99
350, 351.	PREPOSITIONS GOVERNING TWO CASES	100
351–358.	PREPOSITIONS GOVERNING THREE CASES	101
359–375.	THE CONJUNCTIONS	103
360–367.	COÖRDINATING CONJUNCTIONS	103
368–375.	SUBORDINATING CONJUNCTIONS	106

The examples, unless otherwise designated, are taken from Xenophon's *Anabasis*. References to Homer are indicated by large Greek letters (for the books of the *Iliad*) and by small Greek letters (for the books of the *Odyssey*).

ABBREVIATIONS

Aes. = Aeschines.
And. = Andocides.
Ar. = Aristophanes.
Av. = Birds.
Nub. = Clouds.
Dem. = Demosthenes.
Hdt. = Herodotus.
Lys. = Lysias.
Pl. = Plato.
Ap. = Apology.
Cr. = Crito.
G. = Gorgias.

Pl.Ph. = Phaedo.
Prot. = Protagoras.
R. = Republic.
Sym. = Symposium.
Soph. = Sophocles.
O.T. = Oedipus Tyrannus.
Th. = Thucydides.
X. = Xenophon.
C. = Cyropaedia.
H. = Hellenica.
M. = Memorabilia.
S. = Symposium.

BRIEF GREEK SYNTAX

1. **The Concords.** — In the structure of sentences there are four concords.
   a. Of subject and verb.
   b. Of substantive and substantive.
   c. Of substantive and adjective.
   d. Of pronoun and antecedent.

SUBJECT AND VERB

2. **Subject and Verb.** — A verb agrees with its subject in person and number.

Σὺ ... γὰρ Ἕλλην εἶ 2. 1. 16.
For you are a Greek.

Καὶ οὐκέτι τρία ἢ τέτταρα στάδια διειχέτην τὼ φάλαγγε ἀπ' ἀλλήλων 1. 8. 17.
And the lines were now less than three or four stades apart.

Οἱ μὲν στρατηγοὶ παρεκλήθησαν εἴσω 2. 5. 31.
The generals were invited within.

3. **Compound Subject.** — After a subject composed of two or more substantives the verb may be plural, or it may agree with only one of its subjects.

Ταύτην δὴ τὴν πάροδον Κῦρός τε καὶ ἡ στρατιὰ παρῆλθε καὶ ἐγένοντο εἴσω τῆς τάφρου 1. 7. 16.
Now through this passage Cyrus and his army passed and came within the ditch.

4. **Dual and Plural.** — A dual subject may have a plural verb, and a plural subject, denoting in fact a pair, may have a dual verb.

Προσέτρεχον δύο νεανίσκω 4. 3. 10.   Καμέτην δέ μοι ἵπποι Δ 27.
Two youths ran up.   And my horses became tired.

5. A Neuter Plural Subject. — A neuter plural subject regularly takes a singular verb.

Ἐφαίνετο ἴχνη ἵππων 1. 6. 1.   Οὐ γὰρ ἔστι πλοῖα 6. 4. 12.
Horse tracks kept appearing.   For there are no boats.

Cf. Ὑποχωρούντων φανερὰ ἦσαν καὶ ἵππων καὶ ἀνθρώπων ἴχνη πολλά 1. 7. 17.
Many tracks were seen both of horses and men in retreat.

6. A Collective Subject. — Nouns of multitude often take the verb in the plural.

Ὣς φάσαν ἡ πληθύς B 278.
Thus said the multitude.

SUBSTANTIVE AND SUBSTANTIVE

7. Apposition. — A substantive in apposition with another agrees with it in case.

Ὀρόντας δὲ Πέρσης ἀνήρ 1. 6. 1.   Σὺν Πίγρητι τῷ ἑρμηνεῖ 1. 8. 12.
Orontas a Persian.   With Pigres the interpreter.

Καὶ τὸ βασίλειον σημεῖον ὁρᾶν ἔφασαν ἀετόν τινα χρυσοῦν 1. 10. 12.
And they said they saw the royal standard, a kind of golden eagle.

8. Predicate Agreement. — Substantives connected by copulative verbs, particularly εἰμί and γίγνομαι, agree in case (cf. 45, 52).

Κλέαρχος Λακεδαιμόνιος φυγὰς ἦν 1. 1. 9.
Clearchus was a Lacedaemonian exile.

Τὰ δὲ ἆθλα ἦσαν στλεγγίδες χρυσαῖ 1. 2. 10.
And the prizes were golden strigils.

Καὶ ἐγένοντο οἱ σύμπαντες ὁπλῖται ... μύριοι καὶ χίλιοι 1. 2. 9.
And all together amounted to eleven thousand hoplites.

SUBSTANTIVE AND ADJECTIVE

9. Agreement of Attributive Adjective. — The adjective (including the article, pronominal adjectives, and participles) agrees in gender, number, and case with the substantive it modifies.

Τὸν κάλλιστον κόσμον 3. 2. 7.
The fairest ornament.
Πολλαὶ ἡμῖν καὶ καλαὶ ἐλπίδες εἰσὶ σωτηρίας 3. 2. 8.
We have many good hopes of safety.

10. Agreement of Predicate Adjective. — The adjective in the predicate after copulative verbs, especially εἰμί and γίγνομαι, agrees with its substantive in gender, number, and case.

Ἦν γὰρ ἡ πάροδος στενή 1. 4. 4.
For the passage was narrow.
Οὔπω καταφανεῖς ἦσαν οἱ πολέμιοι 1. 8. 8.
The enemy were not yet in sight.
Ἀγαθοῖς ... ὑμῖν προσήκει εἶναι 3. 2. 11.
It befits you to be brave.
Ὁμολογεῖς οὖν περὶ ἐμὲ ἄδικος γεγενῆσθαι; 1. 6. 8.
Do you then admit that you have been unjust toward me? (cf. 45.)

11. Predicate Adjective Neuter. — A predicate adjective is, however, often neuter, being used like a noun without regard to the gender or number of its substantive.

Φοβερώτατον δ' ἐρημία 2. 5. 9.
And a desert is a most fearful thing.
Τοὺς δὲ ποταμοὺς ἄπορον νομίζετε εἶναι 3. 2. 22.
But you regard the rivers as a difficulty.

PRONOUN AND ANTECEDENT

12. Pronoun Agreement. — The pronoun (personal, relative, demonstrative, etc.) agrees with its antecedent in number and gender.

Νῆες τριάκοντα καὶ πέντε καὶ ἐπ' αὐταῖς ναύαρχος 1. 4. 2.
Thirty-five ships and an admiral on board of them.

Ἡμέρας τρεῖς· ἐν αἷς κτέ. 1. 2. 10.
Three days; in which, etc.

Οὔτε γὰρ ἡμεῖς ἐκείνου (Κύρου) ἔτι στρατιῶται, ἐπεί γε οὐ συνεπόμεθα αὐτῷ, οὔτε ἐκεῖνος ἔτι ἡμῖν μισθοδότης 1. 3. 10.
For neither are we his soldiers any longer, since we do not follow him, nor is he any longer our paymaster.

13. Assimilation of Relative. — The relative pronoun may by assimilation take the case of its antecedent.

Ἄξιοι τῆς ἐλευθερίας ἧς κέκτησθε 1. 7. 3 (for ἥν).
Worthy of the freedom you possess.

Δεῖταί σου τήμερον τοῦτον ἐκπιεῖν σὺν οἷς μάλιστα φιλεῖς 1. 9. 25 (= τούτοις οὕς).
He begs you to drink this to-day with those you love most.

14. Incorporation of Antecedent. — The antecedent may be incorporated in the relative clause. This involves assimilation where the cases of antecedent and relative would logically be different.

Οὐκ ἀπεκρύπτετο ἣν εἶχε γνώμην XM 4. 4. 1 (= τὴν γνώμην ἣν εἶχε).
He did not conceal the opinion he had.

Τὴν ἐλευθερίαν ἑλοίμην ἂν ἀνθ' ὧν ἔχω πάντων 1. 7. 3 (= ἀντὶ πάντων ἃ ἔχω).
I should choose freedom in preference to all that I have.

Ἐπορεύετο σὺν ᾗ εἶχε δυνάμει XH 4. 1. 23.
He marched with what force he had.

THE ARTICLE

15. Use of Article. — The definite article is used much as in English.

Εἷλκον δὲ τὰς νευρὰς ὁπότε τοξεύοιεν πρὸς τὸ κάτω τοῦ τόξου τῷ ἀριστερῷ ποδὶ προσβαίνοντες 4. 2. 28.
And when(ever) they shot they drew the strings toward the lower end of the bow advancing the left foot.

16. Article with Proper Names and Abstracts. — Unlike the English usage, the article is allowed with proper names, and is the rule with abstracts.

Ὁ Ξενοφῶν, ὁ Ὅμηρος.   Ἡ σοφία, ἡ ἀλήθεια.
Xenophon ; Homer.   Wisdom ; truth.

17. The Generic Article. — The article is used with class names, both in the singular and in the plural.

Ὁ ἄνθρωπος,   ὁ κύων.
Man (*or* the man) ; the dog (*generic or specific*).
Οἱ ἵπποι.
Horses (*or* the horses).
Τὰς δὲ ὠτίδας, ἄν τις ταχὺ ἀνιστῇ, ἔστι λαμβάνειν 1. 5. 3.
Bustards, if one rouse them suddenly, may be caught.

18. Article with Demonstratives and Possessives. — The article is required in prose with the demonstrative and possessive adjectives (cf. 26).

Οὗτος ὁ ἀνήρ.   Ἐκείνη ἡ γυνή.
This man.   That woman.

Ὁ ἐμὸς πατήρ.   Cf. Ἐμὸς ἀδελφός.
My father.   A brother of mine.

19. Article without a Noun. — The article is used freely with adjectives, adverbs of time, limiting genitives, or prepositional phrases, without a noun, when the latter is readily supplied.

Οἱ φρόνιμοι.   Αἱ σοφαί.
Prudent men.   Wise women.

Ὁ Δαρείου.   Οἱ ἀπὸ τούτων τῶν οἰκιῶν 5. 2. 25.
The (son) of Darius.   The (men) from these houses.

20. Article in Place of Possessive. — An article is often used where the English idiom requires a possessive adjective.

Διαβάλλει τὸν Κῦρον πρὸς τὸν ἀδελφόν 1. 1. 3.
He slanders Cyrus to his brother.
Ἐκπεπτωκότες τῶν οἰκιῶν 5. 2. 1.
Expelled from their houses.

21. Homeric Use. — In Homer ὁ, ἡ, τό is regularly a demonstrative or a relative. In Attic prose the demonstrative force is preserved in ὁ δέ, *and he*, at the beginning of a sentence, and in ὁ μέν ... ὁ δέ, *the one ... the other.*

Ὁ γὰρ βασιλῆι χολωθείς κτέ. A 9.
For he, angered at the king, etc.

Ὁ δὲ πείθεταί τε καὶ συλλαμβάνει Κῦρον 1. 1. 3.
And he was persuaded and arrested Cyrus.

Τοὺς μὲν αὐτῶν ἀπέκτεινε τοὺς δ' ἐξέβαλεν 1. 1. 7.
He killed some of them and banished others.

POSITION OF THE ARTICLE

22. With a Noun. — The article stands before its noun.

Ὁ ἀνήρ.   Ἡ οἰκία.
The man.   The house.

23. Attributive Position. — When the noun has also an attributive adjective, the order is *article, adjective, noun*, or more formally *article, noun, article, adjective*, or sometimes *noun, article, adjective*. This is called the attributive position.

Οἱ δειλοὶ κύνες 3. 2. 35.   Ἡ ἀρχὴ ἡ πατρῴα 1. 7. 6.
Cowardly dogs.   My ancestral realm.

Πόλεμος ὁ μέγας Hdt. 5. 50.
The great war.

24. Predicative Position. — When the adjective belongs to the predicate, the order is *article, noun, adjective*, or *adjective, article, noun*. This is called the predicative position.

Ἡ πάροδος στενή 1. 4. 4.   Ψιλὴν ἔχων τὴν κεφαλήν 1. 8. 6.
The passage was narrow.   With his head bare.

25. With Adjectival Modifiers. — With prepositional phrases and limiting genitives used attributively, the attributive position is common, but not necessary.

Ἡ Συεννέσιος γυνή 1. 2. 12.
The wife of Syennesis.

Κῦρος δὲ ἥσθη τὸν ἐκ τῶν Ἑλλήνων εἰς τοὺς βαρβάρους **φόβον ἰδών**
1. 2. 18.

And Cyrus was pleased when he saw the terror with which the Greeks inspired the barbarians.

Ἐν ταῖς κώμαις ταῖς ὑπὲρ τοῦ πεδίου τοῦ παρὰ τὸν Κεντρίτην ποταμόν
4. 3. 1.

In the villages above the plain along the Centrites river.

Cf. Παρὰ τοὺς στρατηγοὺς τῶν Ἑλλήνων 1. 2. 17.
To the generals of the Greeks.

26. With Possessives and Demonstratives. — With possessive adjectives the attributive position is used, but with demonstratives the predicative position (cf. 18).

Ὁ ἐμὸς πατήρ, ὁ πατὴρ ὁ ἐμός, πατὴρ ὁ ἐμός.
My father.

Οὗτος ὁ ἀνήρ,   ἡ γυνὴ ἐκείνη.
That man;   that woman.

Ἐνίκων οἱ ἡμέτεροι πρόγονοι τοὺς τούτων προγόνους 3. 2. 13.
Our ancestors conquered the ancestors of these men.

Τοὺς τῶν προγόνων τῶν ἡμετέρων κινδύνους 3. 2. 11.
The perils of our ancestors.

Διὰ τούτου τοῦ πεδίου 1. 2. 23.
Through this plain.

Further Uses of the Predicative Position

27. Article with the Possessive Genitive of Personal Pronouns. — The genitive of the personal pronouns used as possessives has the predicative position.

Ὁ πατήρ σου, or σοῦ ὁ πατήρ.   Ὁ δ' ἀνὴρ αὐτῆς 4. 5. 24.
Thy father.   Her husband.

28. Article with ἕκαστος, ἀμφότερος. — Generally ἕκαστος, ἑκάτερος, *each*, and ἄμφω, ἀμφότερος, *both*, have predicative position.

Ἑκάστη ἡ οἰκία.   Οἱ φίλοι ἀμφότεροι.
Each house.   Both friends.

Ἐβούλετο τὼ παῖδε **ἀμφοτέρω** παρεῖναι 1. 1. 1.
He wished both his sons to be present.

Cf. Ἐφ' **ἑκάστης** δὲ προδρομῆς πλέον ἢ δέκα ἅμαξαι πετρῶν ἀνηλίσκοντο
4. 7. 10.

And at each sally more than ten wagon loads of stones were used up.

29. Article with Adjectives of Place.

The adjectives ἄκρος, meaning *the top of*, μέσος, *the middle of*, ἔσχατος, *the extreme of*, have predicative position.

Ἄκρον τὸ ὄρος.
The mountain top.

Ἡ πόλις μέση.
The middle of the city.

Διὰ μέσου δὲ τοῦ παραδείσου ῥεῖ 1. 2. 7.
And it flows through the middle of the park.

Cf. Τοὺς **ἐσχάτους** λόχους 4. 8. 12.
The outermost companies.

Ἡ μέση πόλις.
The middle city.

30. Article with πᾶς, ὅλος.

Generally πᾶς, *all, whole,* and ὅλος, *whole,* have predicative position.

Πᾶσα ἡ πόλις,   cf. **πᾶσα πόλις**.
The whole city;   every city.

Ἡ χώρα ὅλη.
The whole country.

Οἱ δ' ἵπποι **πάντες** οἱ μετὰ Κύρου 1. 8. 7.
And all the horses with Cyrus.

Κατεκαύθη **πᾶσα** ἡ πόλις 5. 2. 27.
The whole city was burnt.

PRONOUNS

31. Personal Pronouns, Nominative.

The nominative of the personal pronouns is not generally used unless it is emphatic. The lack of a nominative third person (cf. 32) is supplied, when necessary, by the various demonstratives, ὁ (in its demonstrative use, cf. 21), οὗτος, or ἐκεῖνος, and by ὅς in the phrase καὶ ὅς, *and he.*

Χαλεπῶς φέρω τοῖς παροῦσι πράγμασιν 1. 3. 3.
I am distressed at the present circumstances.

Ἐγὼ σὺν ὑμῖν ἕψομαι 1. 3. 6.
I will follow along with you.

Οὗτοι μὲν εἰς Σάρδεις ... ἀφίκοντο 1. 2. 4.
Now these came to Sardis.

Καὶ ὃς ἐθαύμασε τίς παραγγέλλει ... τὸ σύνθημα 1. 8. 16.
And he wondered who was giving out the watchword.

32. Αὐτός as Third Personal Pronoun. — The oblique cases of αὐτός (but never at the beginning of a sentence) serve in prose as the forms of the personal pronoun of the third person.

Προδοῦναι αὐτόν 2. 3. 22.
To betray him.

Δικαίως ἔπαιον αὐτούς 5. 8. 21.
I beat them justly.

Ἡ μήτηρ συνέπραττεν αὐτῷ ταῦτα 1. 1. 8.
His mother coöperated with him in this.

33. Αὐτός as Intensive Pronoun. — In the predicative position αὐτός is intensive, meaning *self*. So also when standing by itself in the nominative.

Αὐτὸς ὁ ἀνήρ.
The man himself.

Ἡ γυνὴ αὐτή.
The woman herself.

Περὶ δὲ αὐτὸν τὸν ναόν 5. 3. 12.
And around the temple itself.

Αὐτὸς ὀμόσας ἡμῖν, αὐτὸς δεξιὰς δούς, αὐτὸς ἐξαπατήσας συνέλαβε τοὺς στρατηγούς 3. 2. 4.
Though he swore to us himself, and himself gave pledges, yet he himself deceived and arrested the generals.

34. Ὁ αὐτός, the same. — In the attributive position αὐτός means *same*.

Ὁ αὐτὸς ἀνήρ,
The same man;

ἡ αὐτὴ γυνή,
the same woman;

ταὐτά ταῦτα.
these same things.

Τοὺς αὐτοὺς εὑρήσετε καὶ τότε κακίστους καὶ νῦν ὑβριστοτάτους 5. 8. 22.
You will find the same men then most cowardly and now most insolent.

35. Reflexive Pronouns. — The reflexive pronouns refer to the subject of the clause in which they stand. They are used much as in English, but the forms of the third person are sometimes used for the first and second person, *e.g.* αὐτῶν for ἡμῶν αὐτῶν.

Ἐγὼ δέ σοι ... δίδωμι ἐμαυτόν 7. 3. 30.
But I give you myself.

Βουλεύεσθαι ὑπὲρ ἡμῶν αὐτῶν 5. 7. 12.
To deliberate concerning ourselves.

Δεῖ ἡμᾶς ἀνερέσθαι ἑαυτούς Pl. Ph. 78 b.
We must question ourselves.

36. Indirect Reflexives. — A pronoun in a subordinate clause, which refers to the subject of the principal clause, is called an indirect reflexive. In Attic οὗ οἷ ἕ, etc., are thus used. Occasionally, however, ἑαυτοῦ, etc., and the oblique cases of αὐτός are also used as indirect reflexives.

Ἠξίου ... δοθῆναι οἷ ταύτας τὰς πόλεις 1. 1. 8.
He claimed that these cities should be given to *him*.

Νομίσας ἑτοίμους εἶναι αὐτῷ τοὺς ἱππέας 1. 6. 3.
Thinking that the horsemen were ready for him.

37. Homeric Use. — In Homer ἕο (with the other case-forms) is used as a third personal pronoun (= αὐτοῦ), as a direct reflexive (= ἑαυτοῦ), and as an indirect reflexive (cf. 36)

Καί οἱ πείθονται Ἀχαιοί Α 79.
And the Achaeans obey him.

Ἀχιλῆα, ἕο μέγ' ἀμείνονα φῶτα, | ἠτίμησεν Β 239.
Achilles, a far better man than himself, he dishonored.

38. Possessive Adjectives. — The possessive of the third person is wanting in Attic. Compare ὁ ἐμὸς πατήρ, ὁ πατὴρ ὁ ἐμός, πατὴρ ὁ ἐμός, ὁ πατήρ μου, *my father*, and ὁ πατὴρ αὐτοῦ, *his father*.

Τῷ ἐμῷ ἀδελφῷ πολέμιος 1. 6. 8.
Hostile to my brother.

Περὶ τῶν ὑμετέρων ἀγαθῶν μαχούμεθα 2. 1. 12.
For your property we shall fight.

Τῷ νόμῳ τῷ ὑμετέρῳ πείσομαι 7. 3. 39.
I shall obey your custom.

Τῷ σώματι αὐτοῦ κόσμον 1. 9. 23.
An adornment for his person.

39. Homeric Possessives. — In Homer ὅς, *his, his own*, ἥ, *her, her own*, etc., σφέτερος (σφός), etc., *their, their own*, are the possessive adjectives of the third person.

Αὐτὰρ ὁ ἔγνω ᾗσιν ἐνὶ φρεσί Α 333.
But he understood in his heart.

Ὁ γὰρ αὖτε βίῃ οὗ πατρὸς ἀμείνων Α 404.
For he in turn was mightier than his sire.

Κεῖνοι δὲ σφετέρῃσιν ἀτασθαλίῃσιν ὄλοντο Δ 409.
And they by their infatuation perished.

40. Demonstrative Pronouns. — The chief demonstrative pronouns are οὗτος, ὅδε, *this*, and ἐκεῖνος, *that*. Of these, οὗτος is the ordinary antecedent to the relative. Further, οὗτος refers to something mentioned, ὅδε to something actually present, οὗτος to what precedes, ὅδε to what follows. Cf. οὕτως : ὧδε or τοιοῦτος : τοιόσδε.

Ἐπὶ τούτων διέβαινον 1. 5. 10.
On these (*before mentioned*) they crossed.

Τόνδε τὸν τρόπον 1. 1. 9.   Ἐκείνην τὴν ἡμέραν 2. 1. 6.
In the following manner.   On that day.

41. Relative Pronouns. — The chief relative pronouns are ὅς, *who*, and its compounds ὅστις, *whoever* (indefinite), and ὅσπερ, *the very one who* (specific).

Καὶ ὅτῳ δοκεῖ ταῦτ', ἔφη, ἀνατεινάτω τὴν χεῖρα 3. 2. 9.
And whoever approves of this, said he, let him raise his hand.

Ὅπερ ᾤετο ποιήσειν ὁ Κῦρος 1. 4. 5.
Just what Cyrus thought he would do.

42. Interrogative Pronouns. — The chief interrogatives are τίς; *who?* πόσος; *how great?* ποῖος; *of what sort?* with the corresponding indirect forms ὅστις, ὁπόσος, ὁποῖος. Direct questions require τίς; etc.; indirect questions may have either the direct or the indirect forms (cf. 301).

Ἐθαύμασε τίς παραγγέλλει καὶ ἤρετο ὅ τι εἴη τὸ σύνθημα 1. 8. 16.
He wondered who was giving out the watchword, and asked what it was.

43. Ἄλλος. — Ἄλλος, *another* (*besides, else*), does not necessarily apply merely to that which is of the class or kind mentioned, as the English *another*.

Οὐ γὰρ ἦν χόρτος οὐδὲ ἄλλο οὐδὲν δένδρον 1. 5. 5.
For there was no grass, and besides not a tree.

THE CASES OF THE NOUN
NOMINATIVE

44. Subject Case. — The subject of a finite verb is put in the nominative case.

Κλέαρχος εἶπε 1. 3. 14. Ἄλλος ἀνέστη 1. 3. 16.
Clearchus said. Another rose.

Ταῦτα οἱ αἱρετοὶ ἀναγγέλλουσι τοῖς στρατιώταις 1. 3. 21.
This the delegates report to the soldiers.

45. Predicate Nominative. — The predicate after εἰμί, γίγνομαι, and other copulative verbs (cf. 8) is put in the nominative case.

Αὕτη αὖ ἄλλη πρόφασις ἦν 1. 1. 7. Ἀρκάδες ἐσμέν 6. 1. 30.
This again was another pretext. We are Arcadians.

Ὁ ποταμὸς καλεῖται Μαρσύας 1. 2. 8.
The river is called Marsyas.

46. Independent Nominative. — The nominative is used independently in titles and the like.

Ξενοφῶντος Κύρου Ἀνάβασις.
Xenophon's 'Anabasis of Cyrus.'

Παρηγγύα ὁ Κῦρος σύνθημα Ζεὺς σύμμαχος καὶ ἡγεμών XC 3. 3. 58.
Cyrus gave out as password, 'Zeus, our Ally and Leader.'

71. With Verbs of Endeavor.

Many verbs of endeavor, signifying *to take hold of, touch, claim, aim at, attain, hit, miss, make trial of, begin*, etc., take a genitive object.

Μὴ ἅπτεσθαι τῆς κάρφης 1. 5. 10.
Not to touch the hay.

Ὤιετο δεῖν τούτων τυγχάνειν 2. 6. 18.
He thought it necessary to get these.

Αὑτοῦ ἥμαρτεν 1. 5. 12. Τοῦ λόγου δὲ ἤρχετο 3. 2. 7.
He missed him. And he began his speech.

72. With Verbs of Sensation.

Some verbs of sense perception and mental action, signifying *to taste, smell, hear, perceive, understand, remember, forget, desire, care for, spare, neglect, admire, despise*, etc., take a genitive object.

Βούλεται οὖν καὶ σὲ τούτων γεύσασθαι 1. 9. 26.
He therefore wishes you also to taste these.

Ἀκούουσι βοώντων τῶν στρατιωτῶν 4. 7. 24.
They hear the soldiers shouting.

Μὴ ὥσπερ οἱ λωτοφάγοι ἐπιλαθώμεθα τῆς οἴκαδε ὁδοῦ 3. 2. 25.
Lest, like the lotus-eaters, we forget the way home.

Ἀλλήλων ἐπεμέλοντο 4. 2. 26.
They looked out for each other.

73. With Verbs of Power.

Verbs signifying *to rule, lead, command*, etc., take a genitive object.

Τοῦ δεξιοῦ κέρως ἡγεῖσθαι 1. 7. 1.
To lead the right wing.

Πάντων ἴσον οἱ θεοὶ κρατοῦσι 2. 5. 7.
The gods hold sway over all things alike.

Ἄρχειν δὲ καλῶν μὲν κἀγαθῶν δυνατὸς ἦν 2. 6. 19.
And he was able to command honorable and good men.

74. With Compound Verbs.

Verbs compounded with certain prepositions, especially πρό, περί, and ὑπέρ, may take a genitive depending upon the prepositional notion.

Προβουλεύειν **τούτων** καὶ προπονεῖν 3. 1. 37.
To plan and toil for these.

Ὑπερκάθηνται δ' **ἡμῶν** 5. 1. 9.
And they are stationed above us.

Genitive with Verbs, as Adverbial Modifier

75. With Verbs of Plenty or Want. — Verbs of plenty or want may be followed by a genitive of material (cf. 66).

Ἐπίμπλασαν **χόρτου** κούφου 1. 5. 10.
They filled (the skins) with hay.

Ἐψιλοῦτο δ' ὁ λόφος **τῶν ἱππέων** 1. 10. 13.
And the hill was bared of the horsemen.

76. Genitive of Cause. — Verbs of emotion (joy, grief, anger, etc.) may be followed by a genitive of the cause of the emotion.

Τῆς ἐλευθερίας . . . ἧς ὑμᾶς ἐγὼ εὐδαιμονίζω 1. 7. 3.
Of the freedom on which I congratulate you.

Μὴ μνησικακήσειν βασιλέα αὐτοῖς **τῆς σὺν Κύρῳ ἐπιστρατείας** 2. 4. 1.
That the king would bear them no grudge because of the expedition with Cyrus.

77. Causal Genitive in Exclamation. — In exclamations the causal genitive may be used without any verb expressed.

Εἶπε πρὸς αὐτόν, **τῆς τύχης** XC 2. 2. 3.
He said to himself, 'What a misfortune!'

78. Genitive of Crime. — Verbs of judicial action, signifying *to accuse, acquit, convict, judge, punish,* etc., take an accusative of the person and a genitive of the crime. But compounds of κατά take a genitive of the person and may have also an accusative of the crime.

Τιμωρήσασθαι αὐτοὺς **τῆς ἐπιθέσεως** 7. 4. 23.
To punish them for the attack.

Καταδικάζω **ἐμαυτοῦ** 6. 6. 15.
I condemn myself.

§ 83] GENITIVE

79. Genitive of Separation. — Verbs of separation and distinction, signifying *to be distant, differ, remove, abstain, deprive* (cf. 59), etc., may be followed by the genitive.

Ἀπεῖχον τῆς χαράδρας ὅσον ὀκτὼ σταδίους 3. 4. 3.
They were distant from the ravine about eight stades.

Ἡ δὲ ὄψις ἠλέκτρου οὐδὲν διέφερε 2. 3. 15.
And its appearance did not differ at all from amber.

Ποδῶν καὶ χειρῶν καὶ ὀφθαλμῶν στερομένους ἀνθρώπους 1. 9. 13.
Men deprived of feet, hands, and eyes.

80. Genitive of Comparison. — Verbs of superiority and inferiority may be followed by the genitive of comparison.

Τὸ δὲ τῇ ἐπιμελείᾳ περιεῖναι τῶν φίλων 1. 9. 24.
His surpassing his friends in thoughtfulness.

Ἀβροκόμας δὲ ὑστέρησε τῆς μάχης 1. 7. 12.
But Abrocomas came too late for the battle.

81. Genitive of Source. — Many verbs may be followed by a genitive of source.

Μάθε δέ μου καὶ τάδε XC 1. 6. 44.
And learn from me this also.

Τούτων καὶ πυνθάνομαι ὅτι οὐκ ἄβατόν ἐστι τὸ ὄρος 4. 6. 17.
From these I ascertain also that the mountain is not impassable.

Τοιούτων μέν ἐστε προγόνων 3. 2. 13.
Of such ancestors are ye.

82. Genitive of Price. — Verbs of buying, selling, appraising, and the like, may be followed by a genitive of the price.

Ἀπέδοτο πεντήκοντα δαρεικῶν 7. 8. 6.
He sold it for fifty darics.

Μικρὰ μέτρα πολλοῦ ἀργυρίου 3. 2. 21.
Scant measure for much money.

83. Genitive of Time. — The genitive may express the time (in poetry also the place) within which an action takes place.

Βασιλεὺς οὐ μαχεῖται δέκα ἡμερῶν 1. 7. 18.
The king will not fight within ten days.

Οὔπω δὴ πολλοῦ χρόνου 1. 9. 25.
Not for (within) a long time.

Γίγνεται τῆς νυκτὸς χιὼν πολλή 4. 4. 8.
Much snow fell during the night.

Genitive with Adjectives and Adverbs

84. Of Endeavor, Sensation, Power, Plenty, Want, etc. — The genitive may depend on adjectives and adverbs of meaning akin to that of verbs which take a genitive.

Τῶν ἐμπείρως αὐτοῦ ἐχόντων 2. 6. 1 (cf. 71).
Of those acquainted with him.

Λάθρᾳ τῶν στρατιωτῶν 1. 3. 8 (cf. 72).
Without the knowledge of the soldiers.

Ἀγρίων θηρίων πλήρης 1. 2. 7. (cf. 75).
Full of wild beasts.

Θαυμάσιαι τοῦ κάλλους καὶ μεγέθους 2. 3. 15 (cf. 76).
Marvelous for beauty and size.

Ἄξιοι τῆς ἐλευθερίας 1. 7. 3.
Worthy of freedom.

85. With Adjectives of Transitive Action. — Some adjectives of transitive action take an objective genitive.

Ἔκρινον δ' αὐτὸν καὶ τῶν εἰς τὸν πόλεμον ἔργων, τοξικῆς τε καὶ ἀκοντίσεως, φιλομαθέστατον καὶ μελετηρότατον 1. 9. 5.
And they judged him to be most eager to learn and practice also the arts of war, both archery and javelin throwing.

Ἐπιστήμων . . . τῶν ἀμφὶ τάξεις 2. 1. 7.
Skilled in military tactics.

86. Genitive after Comparatives. — The genitive is used after the comparative degree of adjectives or adverbs (cf. the use of ἤ, *than*, 363).

Ἦσαν δ' οἱ ταύτῃ ἵπποι μείονες μὲν τῶν Περσικῶν 4. 5. 36.
And the horses here were smaller than the Persian horses.

Πολὺ γὰρ τῶν ἵππων ἔτρεχον θᾶττον 1. 5. 2.
For they ran much faster than the horses.

87. With Adverbs of Place. — The genitive is used with adverbs of place, such as εἴσω, *within;* ἔξω, ἐκτός, *outside;* πέραν, *beyond;* ποῦ, *where.*

Εἴσω τῆς τάφρου 1. 7. 16.   Ἐγγὺς παραδείσου 2. 4. 14.
Within the ditch.   Near a park.

Ἧι ἕκαστος ἐτύγχανε τοῦ νάπους ὤν 6. 5. 22.
At whatever part of the glen each one chanced to be.

88. Genitive Absolute. — A noun and a participle may stand together in the genitive absolute (cf. 277).

Κελεύοντος Κύρου 1. 6. 10.
At the bidding of Cyrus.

DATIVE

89. Dative, Instrumental, and Locative. — The dative has three fundamental meanings, that of the true dative, the remoter object (*to* or *for*), that of the lost instrumental, whose place it has taken, denoting means, instrument, etc. (*with* or *by*), and that of the lost locative, of place or time (*in* or *at*). In most of its uses this distinction is quite clear.

90. Indirect Object. — The indirect object of a transitive verb is put in the dative.

Ὁ δὲ Κῦρος ὑπισχνεῖται ἡμιόλιον πᾶσι δώσειν οὗ πρότερον ἔφερον 1. 3. 21.
And Cyrus promised to give to all half as much again as they had been receiving before.

Ταῦτα οἱ αἱρετοὶ ἀναγγέλλουσι τοῖς στρατιώταις 1. 3. 21.
This the delegates report to the soldiers.

Ὑπισχνοῦμαι ὑμῖν τὴν μισθοφοράν 5. 6. 26.
I promise you your pay.

91. Dative Object of Intransitives. — Many intransitive verbs, some of which are transitive in English, take a dative object. Such are those meaning *to befit, belong, benefit, serve, obey, assist, trust, abuse, threaten, be angry*, etc.

Ἐβοήθουν ἀλλήλοις 4. 2. 26.
They aided each other.

Τῇ ἡλικίᾳ ἔπρεπε 1. 9. 6.
It suited his time of life.

Ἐπίστευον γὰρ αὐτῷ 1. 2. 2.
For they trusted him.

Ἀλλ' ἠπείλουν αὐτῷ 5. 6. 34.
But they threatened him.

Οἱ δὲ στρατιῶται ἐχαλέπαινον τοῖς στρατηγοῖς 1. 4. 12.
But the soldiers were angry with the generals.

92. Dative of Advantage or Disadvantage. — Almost any verb may be followed by the dative of the person (or thing) for whom something is done.

Ἄλλο δὲ στράτευμα αὐτῷ συνελέγετο 1. 1. 9.
And another army was being collected for him.

Ἡρώτων τίνι οἱ ἵπποι τρέφοιντο 4. 5. 34.
They asked for whom the horses were bred.

Αἱ βάλανοι τῶν φοινίκων ... τοῖς οἰκέταις ἀπέκειντο 2. 3. 15.
The dates were laid aside for the slaves.

93. Ethical Dative. — The person whose feelings sympathize with the action may be added in the dative. This is often scarcely to be translated.

Τί σοι μαθήσομαι Ar. Nub. 111.
What would you have me learn?

Σωφροσύνης ἆρα οὐ δεήσει ἡμῖν τοῖς νεανίαις Pl. R. 389 d.
Will not our young men stand in need of temperance?

94. Dative of Possessor. — The dative of the possessor is used in the predicate after εἰμί and γίγνομαι (cf. 69).

Αὕτη αὖ ἄλλη πρόφασις ἦν αὐτῷ 1. 1. 7.
In this he had another pretext.

Δρόμος ἐγένετο τοῖς στρατιώταις 1. 2. 17.
The soldiers began to run.

Τί ἔσται τοῖς στρατιώταις; 2. 1. 10.
What will the soldiers have?

95. Dative with Compounds. — The dative is used as object of many compound verbs, especially those with ἐν, σύν, ἐπί, and some with πρός, παρά, περί, ὑπό.

Τοῖς Ἕλλησι φόβος ἐμπίπτει 2. 2. 19.
Fear falls on the Greeks.

Ἐπιβουλεύει Κύρῳ 1. 6. 1.
He plots against Cyrus.

Καὶ συνέπεμψεν αὐτῇ στρατιώτας 1. 2. 20.
And he sent soldiers with her.

Αὐτοῖς προσελθών τις 3. 5. 8.
Some one coming up to them.

96. Dative of Union or Opposition. — The dative follows verbs of union, approach, association, or opposition.

Πολὺν χρόνον διαλεχθέντες ἀλλήλοις ἀπῆλθον 2. 5. 42.
After conversing a long time with one another they departed.

Ἀπήντησαν αὐτοῖς οἱ τῶν Ἑλλήνων στρατηγοί 2. 3. 17.
The generals of the Greeks met them.

Οὐδεὶς αὐτῷ ἐμάχετο 1. 8. 23.
No one fought with him.

97. Dative of Likeness or Unlikeness. — The dative follows verbs, adjectives, and adverbs, of likeness or unlikeness (cf. 105).

Φιλοσόφῳ μὲν ἔοικας 2. 1. 13.
You resemble a philosopher.

Πορεία ὁμοία φυγῇ 4. 1. 17.
A march like a flight.

Τὸ ὁμοιοῦν ἑαυτὸν ἄλλῳ μιμεῖσθαί ἐστι Pl. R. 393 c.
To liken oneself to another is to imitate.

98. Dative of Cause, Means, Instrument. — The dative is used to denote the cause, means, or instrument.

Ῥίγει ἀπωλλύμεθα 5. 8. 2.
We perished with cold.

Σχεδίαις διαβαίνοντες 1. 5. 10.
Crossing by rafts.

Ὠικοδόμητο δὲ πλίνθοις 3. 4. 7.
It had been built of bricks.

Καὶ ἀποκτεῖναι λέγεται αὐτὸς τῇ ἑαυτοῦ χειρὶ Ἀρταγέρσην 1. 8. 24.
And he is said to have slain Artagerses with his own hand.

99. Dative of Manner or Respect. — The dative is used to denote manner, or the respect in which something is true. The latter is particularly frequent with adjectives (cf. 54).

Δρόμῳ θεῖν 1. 8. 18.   Κραυγῇ πολλῇ ἐπίασιν 1. 7. 4.
To go on a run.   They attack with a great shout.
Ἰσχύειν τοῖς σώμασι XM 2. 7. 7.
To be strong in their bodies.

Γένει τε προσήκων τῷ βασιλεῖ καὶ τὰ πολέμια λεγόμενος ἐν τοῖς ἀρίστοις Περσῶν 1. 6. 1.
Both related in family to the king and reckoned in military matters among the best of the Persians.

100. Dative of Agent. — The dative of the agent (cf. 118) is used after the verbal in -τέος (cf. 291), and sometimes after the perfect and pluperfect passive.

Ἐμοὶ τοῦτο οὐ ποιητέον 1. 3. 15.   Πάνθ' ἡμῖν πεποίηται 1. 8. 12.
I must not do this.   Our whole task is done.

101. Dative of Accompaniment. — The dative of accompaniment is used chiefly in military phrases. In general a preposition is required.

Ὀλίγῳ μὲν γὰρ στρατεύματι οὐ τολμήσει ἐφέπεσθαι 2. 2. 12.
For with a small army he will not dare to follow.

102. Dative of Degree of Difference. — After words containing a notion of comparison the dative expresses the degree of difference.

Ἀβροκόμας δὲ ὑστέρησε τῆς μάχης πέντε ἡμέραις 1. 7. 12.
But Abrocomas came five days too late for the battle.

103. Dative of Time. — The dative is used to express time *when*, chiefly of *day, night, month, year*, and *names of festivals*.

Τῇ δὲ αὐτῇ ἡμέρᾳ 1. 5. 12.   Δῆλον δὲ τοῦτο τῇ ὑστεραίᾳ ἐγένετο 2. 2. 18.
And the same day.   And this became evident the next day.

104. The Dative of Place. — The dative in poetry may express place *where*. In prose some local datives remain as adverbs, as ταύτῃ, *here*, κύκλῳ, *in a circle*.

Τόξ' ὤμοισιν ἔχων A 45.
With a bow on his shoulders.

Πυρὰ πολλὰ ἔκαον κύκλῳ ἐπὶ τῶν ὀρέων 4. 1. 11.
They burned many camp fires round about on the mountains.

105. The Dative with Adjectives, etc. — The dative is used freely with adjectives, adverbs, and verbal nouns to express relations similar to those with verbs.

Τοῖς θεοῖς ὕποχα 2. 5. 7.
Subject to the gods.

Αὐτῷ μᾶλλον φίλους εἶναι ἢ βασιλεῖ 1. 1. 5.
To be friends to him rather than to the king.

Κύρῳ πιστὸς . . . ὑμῖν εὔνους 3. 3. 2.
Faithful to Cyrus, well-disposed to you.

Ἡ πορεία ὁμοία φυγῇ ἐγίγνετο 4. 1. 17.
The march became like a flight.

Τὰ δὲ κρέα . . . ἦν παραπλήσια τοῖς ἐλαφείοις 1. 5. 2.
And the flesh was like venison.

Τὸ αὐτὸ τῷ ἠλιθίῳ 2. 6. 22.   Ἅμα δὲ τῇ ἡμέρᾳ 2. 1. 2.
The same as foolishness.   But at daybreak.

Τῇ φωνῇ τραχύς 2. 6. 9.   Ταῖς ψυχαῖς ἐρρωμεν.στεροι 3. 1. 42.
Harsh in voice.   Firmer in their spirits.

Πλήθει μὲν χώρας καὶ ἀνθρώπων ἰσχυρὰ οὖσα 1. 5. 9.
Being strong in extent of territory and number of men.

Προτέρα Κύρου πέντε ἡμέραις εἰς Ταρσοὺς ἀφίκετο 1. 2. 25.
She arrived at Tarsus five days before Cyrus.

Νομίζων, ὅσῳ μὲν θᾶττον ἔλθοι, τοσούτῳ ἀπαρασκευοτέρῳ βασιλεῖ μαχεῖσθαι 1. 5. 9.
Thinking that the quicker he came, the more unprepared the king would be to fight.

THE VERB

THE VOICES: ACTIVE, MIDDLE, AND PASSIVE

106. The Active Voice. — In the active voice the action proceeds from the subject.

Τισσαφέρνης διαβάλλει τὸν Κῦρον 1. 1. 3.
Tissaphernes slanders Cyrus.

107. The Middle Voice. — In the middle voice the subject is not only the agent, but is concerned in the action, usually as a direct or indirect object.

Πῦρ ἔκαον καὶ ἐχρίοντο 4. 4. 12.
They kindled a fire and anointed themselves.

Τὸ δὲ στράτευμα ἐπορίζετο σῖτον ὅπως ἐδύνατο 2. 1. 6.
And the army procured food for itself as it could.

108. The Passive Voice. — In the passive voice the subject is represented as acted upon.

Στράτευμα αὐτῷ συνελέγετο 1. 1. 9.
An army was being collected for him.

Τρίποδες εἰσηνέχθησαν 7. 3. 21.
Stools were brought in.

Uses of the Middle Voice

109. Directly Reflexive Middle. — The middle, in its most obvious sense, is a direct reflexive.

Λούομαι.   Ἀπάγξασθαι.
I wash myself.   To hang oneself.

Δείσας μὴ ἐφ᾽ ἁρπαγὴν τράποιτο τὸ στράτευμα 7. 1. 18.
Fearing lest the army might betake itself to plunder.

THE VOICES

110. Indirectly Reflexive Middle. — More commonly the reflexive notion *self* is an indirect object.

Μένειν τε αὐτὸν ἐκέλευσε καὶ σύνδειπνον ἐποιήσατο 2. 5. 27.
He invited him to remain and made him his guest.

Ἐνταῦθα ἔμειναν ἡμέρας τρεῖς καὶ ἐπεσιτίσαντο 1. 4. 19.
There they remained three days and procured supplies for themselves.

111. Reciprocal Middle. — The middle is sometimes used in the plural in a reciprocal rather than a reflexive sense.

Ταῦτα συνθέμενοι . . . ἐπορεύοντο 4. 2. 2.
When they had made these agreements with one another, they proceeded.

Διαθέμενοι τὸν σῖτον ὃν ἦσαν συγκεκομισμένοι 6. 6. 37.
Disposing to one another of the food which they had gathered.

112. Special Cases. — In many verbs the reflexive sense is nearly or quite lost, and special differences in meaning have developed between the active and middle forms, *e.g.*

Ἀποδίδωμι.	Ἀποδίδομαι.
I give back.	I sell.
Δανείζειν.	Δανείζεσθαι.
To lend.	To borrow.
Μισθῶ.	Μισθοῦμαι.
I let.	I hire.
Ἔγημε.	Ἐγήματο.
He got married.	She got married.
Πείθειν.	Πείθεσθαι.
To persuade.	To obey.

113. Future Middle as Passive. — The future middle is often used in a passive sense, in some verbs to the exclusion of the future passive (cf. 123).

Οὐδὲ τούτων στερήσονται 1. 4. 8.
Not even of these shall they be deprived.

Concerning the Passive Voice

114. Passive of Verbs that govern the Genitive or Dative. — Many intransitive verbs are used in the passive, the genitive or dative object of the active becoming the subject of the passive.

Ἄρχεσθαι ἐπίσταμαι 1. 3. 15 (cf. 73).
I know how to be ruled.

Ἐπιστευόμην δὲ ὑπὸ Λακεδαιμονίων 7. 6. 33 (cf. 91).
And I was trusted by the Lacedaemonians.

115. Passive of Verbs of Asking, Teaching, etc. — Verbs which, in the active, take an accusative of the person and of the thing, retain in the passive the accusative of the thing, while the accusative of the person becomes the subject (cf. 59).

Διῄρηται δὲ αὕτη ἡ ἀγορὰ . . . τέτταρα μέρη XC 1. 2. 4.
And this market is divided into four parts.

Ἐλέγετο γὰρ καὶ πρόσθεν Τήρης . . . τὰ σκευοφόρα ἀφαιρεθῆναι 7. 2. 22.
For it was said that Teres had even before this been deprived of his pack animals.

116. Passive of Verbs of Naming, Choosing, etc. — Verbs which, in the active, take an object and a predicate accusative, have, in the passive, a subject and a predicate nominative like copulative verbs (cf. 61).

Ἵππαρχος δὲ ἐπεστάθη Λύκιος 3. 3. 20.
And Lycius was appointed cavalry commander.

Δεινὸς νομιζόμενος εἶναι λέγειν 5. 5. 7.
Reputed to be eloquent.

117. Intransitive Actives as Passives. — Some intransitive verbs have become associated as passives with particular transitives, *e.g.*

Ἀποθνῄσκω.   Ἀποκτείνω.
Die, be killed.   Kill.

Πίπτω.	Βάλλω.
Fall, be thrown.	Throw.
Φεύγω.	Διώκω.
Flee, be pursued.	Pursue.
Εὖ πάσχω.	Εὖ ποιῶ.
Fare well, be benefited.	Benefit.
Εὖ ἀκούω.	Εὖ λέγω.
Be well spoken of.	Speak well of.

Ἀπέθανεν ὑπὸ Νικάνδρου 5. 1. 15.
He was killed by Nicander.

Εὖ ἔπαθον ὑπ' ἐκείνου 1. 3. 4.
I was benefited by him.

Μέγα δὲ εὖ ἀκούειν ὑπὸ ἑξακισχιλίων ἀνθρώπων 7. 7. 23.
And it is a great thing to be well spoken of by six thousand men.

Agency with the Passive

118. Agent with Ὑπό. — The agent after passive verbs is regularly expressed by ὑπό with the genitive (cf. 100, 291).

Ἀδικεῖσθαι νομίζει ὑφ' ἡμῶν 1. 3. 10.
He thinks himself wronged by us.

Περιερρεῖτο δ' αὕτη ὑπὸ τοῦ Μάσκα 1. 5. 4.
And this was encircled by the Mascas.

119. Agent with Ἐκ. — The preposition ἐκ, when used with the agent after passive verbs, retains the notion of source (cf. 345).

Πόλεις . . . ἐκ βασιλέως δεδομέναι 1. 1. 6.
Cities given by (a gift from) the king.

120. Agent with Πρός or Παρά. — Both πρός (cf. 357) and παρά (cf. 355) are occasionally used with the agent after passive verbs, retaining more or less of their distinctive meaning.

Ὁμολογεῖται πρὸς πάντων κράτιστος δὴ γενέσθαι θεραπεύειν (φίλους) 1. 9. 20.
He is acknowledged by all to have been best in serving (friends).

Ὡς παρὰ πάντων ὁμολογεῖται 1. 9. 1.
As is acknowledged on all hands.

The Tenses of the Indicative

Classification

121. Period of the Action. — The tenses are classified in accordance with the period of the action, as *past, present,* or *future*. Those of the present or future are called *primary* (or *principal*) tenses, those of the past *secondary* (or *historical*) tenses.

Past: ἔγραφον, ἔγραψα, ἐγεγράφη.
Present: γράφω, γέγραφα.
Future: γράψω, γεγραφὼς ἔσομαι.

122. Stage of the Action. — The tenses also express the stage of the action, distinguishing *continuance, attainment,* and *completion*. There are but seven tenses, for *in form* continuance and attainment are regularly differentiated only in the past.

Continuance: ἔγραφον, γράφω, γράψω.
Attainment: ἔγραψα, γράφω, γράψω.
Completion: ἐγεγράφη, γέγραφα, γεγραφὼς ἔσομαι.

123. Classification Table. — The above classification may be tabulated as follows: —

The Active Voice

	Secondary	Primary	
	Past	Present	Future
Continuance:	ἔγραφον I was writing	γράφω I am writing	γράψω I shall be writing
Attainment:	ἔγραψα I wrote	γράφω I write	γράψω I shall write
Completion:	ἐγεγράφη I had written	γέγραφα I have written	γεγραφὼς ἔσομαι I shall have written

The Passive Voice

	Secondary	Primary	
	Past	Present	Future
Continuance:	ἐγράφετο it was (being) written	γράφεται it is (being) written	γράψεται (cf. 113) it will be written (writing)
Attainment:	ἐγράφη it was written	it is written	γραφήσεται it will be written
Completion:	ἐγέγραπτο it had been written	γέγραπται it has been written	γεγράψεται it will have been written

THE PRESENT TENSE

124. Specific Present. — The present represents an action as going on at the present time.

Νῦν ἐγὼ θαρρῶ σὺν τοῖς θεοῖς μᾶλλον ἢ τότε καὶ θρασύτερός εἰμι νῦν ἢ τότε καὶ οἶνον πλείω πίνω, ἀλλ' ὅμως οὐδένα παίω 5. 8. 19.

Now with the favor of the gods I am more confident than then, and I am bolder now than then, and I drink more wine, but nevertheless I do not strike any one.

125. Universal Present. — The present also expresses a general truth.

Οἱ ἰατροὶ κάουσι καὶ τέμνουσι ἐπ' ἀγαθῷ 5. 8. 18.
Doctors burn and cut for one's good.

Οἱ δειλοὶ κύνες τοὺς μὲν παριόντας διώκουσί τε καὶ δάκνουσι, ἢν δύνωνται 3. 2. 35.

Cowardly dogs chase and bite passers-by if they can.

126. Conative Present. — The present may represent an action as attempted merely, and not actually taking place (cf. 133). This is very common with δίδωμι, *give*, or *offer;* πείθω, *persuade*, or *try to persuade.*

Νῦν δὴ ἐξελαύνετε ἡμᾶς ἐκ τῆσδε τῆς χώρας 7. 7. 7.
So now you are trying to drive us out of this land.

127. Prophetic Present. — The present is sometimes used by lively anticipation for the future.

Τῇ γὰρ στρατιᾷ οὐκ ἔστι τὰ ἐπιτήδεια, εἰ μὴ ληψόμεθα τὸ χωρίον 4. 7. 3.
For the army will not have provisions, unless we capture the place.

128. Present of Εἶμι. — The present of εἶμι, *go* (with its compounds), is regularly future in sense. Ἐλεύσομαι is poetic.

Οὐκ ἐμβησόμεθα; οὐκ ἔξιμεν αὐτοί; Dem. 4. 44.
Shall we not embark, shall we not ourselves go forth?

Σεῦ ὕστερος εἶμ' ὑπὸ γαῖαν Ρ 333.
After you I shall go beneath the earth.

129. Historical Present. — The present may be used in lively narration to express a past action.

Ὡς εἶδε Κλέαρχον διελαύνοντα, ἵησι τῇ ἀξίνῃ 1. 5. 12.
When he saw Clearchus riding through, he hurled his ax at him.

Τοῦτο δὲ λέγοντος αὐτοῦ **πτάρνυταί** τις 3. 2. 9.
As he said this, somebody sneezed.

130. Present for Perfect with Expressions of Time. — The present is often used to express an action begun in the past and continued in the present, especially with πάλαι or other expressions of time (cf. 135).

Εἶναι ἔνθα πάλαι σπεύδομεν 4. 8. 14.
To be where we have long been hastening.

Οὐ πάλαι σοι λέγω; Pl. G. 489 c.
Have I not long ago told you?

131. Presents with Perfect Meaning. — Some presents have a perfect meaning, especially ἥκω, *I have come*, and οἴχομαι, *I am gone*.

Οἶδα γὰρ ὅπῃ οἴχονται 1. 4. 8.
For I know where they have gone.

Τηλόθεν ἥκω Ε 478.
I have come from far.

THE IMPERFECT TENSE

132. Imperfect a Continuative Past. — The imperfect tense regularly expresses continued, repeated, or habitual past action.

Καὶ πρῶτον μὲν ἐδάκρυε πολὺν χρόνον ἑστώς· οἱ δὲ ὁρῶντες ἐθαύμαζον καὶ ἐσιώπων 1. 3. 2.

And first he stood and wept a long time; and seeing him they marveled and kept silence.

Ταῦτα δὲ τὰ θηρία οἱ ἵπποι ἐνίοτε ἐδίωκον 1. 5. 2.

And these wild animals the horses sometimes pursued.

Ὄνους ἀλέτας ... εἰς βαβυλῶνα ἦγον καὶ ἐπώλουν 1. 5. 5.

They were wont to take millstones to Babylon and sell them.

133. Conative Imperfect. — The imperfect may represent a past action as attempted (cf. 126). Especially common in this use are δίδωμι and πείθω.

Ἕκαστος ἔπειθεν αὐτὸν ὑποστῆναι τὴν ἀρχήν 6. 1. 19.

Each one tried to persuade him to undertake the command.

Κλέαρχος τοὺς αὑτοῦ στρατιώτας ἐβιάζετο ἰέναι 1. 3. 1.

Clearchus tried to compel his own soldiers to march.

134. Negative Imperfect. — The imperfect with the negative often implies resistance, and is to be translated *would not* rather than *did not*.

Οἱ δ᾽ αὖ βάρβαροι οὐκ ἐδέχοντο, ἀλλ᾽ ἐκ πλείονος ☙ τὸ πρόσθεν ἔφευγον 1. 10. 11.

And again the barbarians would not await their charge, but began to flee sooner than before.

135. Imperfect for Pluperfect. — The imperfect is often used with πάλαι or other expressions of time to express an action begun in a remoter past and continued in the past (cf. 130).

Οἱ ἄνδρες ἀπῆσαν χρόνον πολλόν Hdt. 4. 1.

Their husbands had been absent a long time.

136. Imperfects with Pluperfect Meaning. — Some imperfects have a pluperfect meaning, especially ἧκον, *I had come*, and ᾠχόμην, *I had gone* (cf. 131).

Κῦρος δὲ οὔπω ἧκεν, ἀλλ᾽ ἔτι προσήλαυνε 1. 5. 12.

Cyrus had not yet come, but was still riding up.

For the modal uses of the imperfect in conditions, wishes, and final clauses, and for the iterative sense with ἄν, see 207, 208, 210, 328.

THE PERFECT TENSE

137. Tense of Completed Action. — The perfect tense expresses an action as completed in the present.

Τετελεύτηκεν 2. 1. 4.
He has died (is dead).

Οἱ πολέμιοι συνειλεγμένοι εἰσὶ καὶ ἀνάγκη μάχεσθαι 6. 4. 21.
The enemy have (are) assembled, and it is necessary to fight.

138. Perfect of Resulting Condition. — Many perfects have become practically presents of a resulting condition (cf. 142).

Μέμνημαι.   Κέκτημαι.
I have recalled, I remember.   I have acquired, I possess.

Ἕστηκα.
I stand.

Σύγε οὐδὲ ὁρῶν γιγνώσκεις οὐδὲ ἀκούων μέμνησαι 3. 1. 27.
As for you, not even when you see do you understand, nor when you hear do you remember.

Ἄξιοι τῆς ἐλευθερίας ἧς κέκτησθε 1. 7. 3.
Worthy of the freedom you possess.

Στήλη ἕστηκε παρὰ τὸν ναόν 5. 3. 13.
A pillar stands by the temple.

Ἀπείρηκα ἤδη συσκευαζόμενος 5. 1. 2.
I am tired now of packing.

139. Intensive Perfect. — The perfect of some verbs is used as an intensive present, especially verbs of *sound, emotion,* and *sight* (cf. 143).

Λαβὼν μὲν σεσίγηκας, ἀναλώσας δὲ κέκραγας Aes. 3. 218.
When you get money you are silent, when you have spent it you cry aloud.

140. Gnomic Perfect. — The perfect may be used, as in English, to express a general truth based on experience.

Ἡ μὲν γὰρ εὐταξία σῴζειν δοκεῖ, ἡ δὲ ἀταξία πολλοὺς ἤδη **ἀπολώλεκεν**
3. 1. 38.

For discipline seems to save, but the lack of it has already destroyed many.

THE PLUPERFECT TENSE

141. Tense of Completed Past Action. — The pluperfect expresses an action as completed in the past.

Ἐτετίμητο γὰρ ὑπὸ Κύρου 1. 8. 29.
For he had been honored by Cyrus.

Κατετέτμηντο δὲ ἐξ αὐτῶν καὶ τάφροι 2. 4. 13.
And from them ditches also had been dug.

142. Pluperfect of Resulting Condition. — Many pluperfects have become practically imperfects of a resulting condition (cf. 138).

Καὶ οἱ μὲν ὄνοι, ἐπεί τις διώκοι, προδραμόντες **ἕστασαν** 1. 5. 2.
And the asses, when pursued, ran on ahead and stopped.

Οἱ δὲ πολέμιοι, ἐπεὶ ᾔσθοντο ἐχόμενον τὸ ὄρος, **ἐγρηγόρεσαν** καὶ ἔκαον πυρὰ πολλὰ διὰ νυκτός 4. 6. 22.
And the enemy, when they perceived that the mountain was occupied, kept vigil and kindled many camp fires through the night.

143. Intensive Pluperfect. — The pluperfect of some verbs is used as an intensive imperfect, especially verbs of *sound, emotion,* and *sight* (cf. 139).

Πάντες μὲν γὰρ ἅμα **ἐκεκράγετε** XC 1. 3. 10.
For you all cried out at once.

THE AORIST TENSE

144. Tense of Simple Past Occurrence. — The aorist tense expresses simple occurrence in the past (attainment).

Ἐπεὶ δὲ **εἶδον** αὐτὸν οἵπερ πρόσθεν προσεκύνουν, καὶ τότε **προσεκύνησαν**
1. 6. 10.

And when those saw him who before were wont to do him homage, they even then did him homage.

Στρουθὸν δὲ οὐδεὶς ἔλαβεν 1. 5. 3.
But no one caught an ostrich.
Ἐκ τούτου ᾑρέθησαν ἄρχοντες 3. 1. 47.
After this leaders were chosen.

145. Ingressive Aorist. — The aorist of verbs expressing a state or condition may denote entrance into that state or condition.

Ἐνόσησε ὁ Ἀλυάττης Hdt. 1. 19.
Alyattes fell sick.
Οὕτω μὲν ἐπλούτησε ἡ οἰκίη αὕτη Hdt. 6. 125.
Thus this house grew rich.

146. Aorist for Perfect. — The aorist is used as a convenient substitute for the perfect where a verb has no perfect in common use, or where the perfect has a special sense (cf. 138, 139).

Τί φῄς; τίς γλαῦκ' Ἀθήναζ' ἤγαγε; Ar. Av. 301.
What say you? Who has brought an owl to Athens?
Πολλάκις ἐθαύμασα XM 1. 1. 1.
I have often wondered.

147. Aorist for Pluperfect. — The aorist is frequently used where the English idiom requires a pluperfect. This is especially common in temporal clauses, and in indirect discourse introduced by ὅτι or ὡς.

Τοῦτο τὸ χρυσίον τότε ἀπέδωκεν, ἐπεὶ **παρῆλθον** αἱ δέκα ἡμέραι 1. 7. 18.
Then he paid this money when the ten days had elapsed.
Διηγεῖται τὸν τρόπον καὶ ὅτι λόχον ποτὲ **συνελέξατο** 7. 4. 8.
He told of his character and that he had once collected a company.
Ἑπτὰ γὰρ ἡμέρας ὅσασπερ ἐπορεύθησαν διὰ τῶν Καρδούχων πάσας μαχόμενοι **διετέλεσαν**, καὶ **ἔπαθον** κακὰ ὅσα οὐδὲ τὰ σύμπαντα ὑπὸ βασιλέως 4. 3. 2.
For all seven days that they had marched through the land of the
  Carduchians they had passed in fighting, and had suffered greater
  evils than all those (they had suffered) at the hands of the king.

148. Gnomic Aorist.
The aorist may express a general truth, or a frequentative action. It is then to be translated by the present.

Ἂν δέ τις τούτων τι παραβαίνῃ, ζημίαν αὐτοῖς ἐπέθεσαν XC 1. 2. 2.
And if one of them transgresses at all, they impose a penalty on him.

Ἤριπε δ' ὡς ὅτε τις δρῦς ἤριπεν N 389.
And he fell as when an oak falls.

149. Impatient Aorist.
The aorist is used for a present in impatient questions.

Τί οὖν οὐ διηγήσω ἡμῖν τὴν ξυνουσίαν; Pl. Prot. 310 a.
Why don't you tell us of the meeting?

150. Dramatic Aorist.
The aorist may be used in dialogue of that which has just been said. It must be translated by the present.

Ὡς ὤνησας, ὅτι μόγις ἀπεκρίνω ὑπὸ τουτωνὶ ἀναγκαζόμενος Pl. Ap. 27 c.
How kind of you to reply (how you oblige me because you reply) reluctantly and under compulsion at their hands!

For the modal uses of the aorist in conditions, wishes, and final clauses, and for the iterative sense with ἄν, see 207, 208, 210, 328.

THE FUTURE TENSE

151. Action about to take Place.
The future represents an action as about to take place. It may denote either continuance or attainment.

Γράψω.
I shall be writing, I shall write.
I will be writing, I will write.

Ἐγὼ δὲ αὐτίκα ἥξω 2. 1. 9.
And I will return presently.

Εἰ μὲν δὴ δίκαια ποιήσω οὐκ οἶδα, αἱρήσομαι δ' οὖν ὑμᾶς 1. 3. 5.
Whether indeed I shall be doing right I know not, but at any rate I shall choose you.

152. Jussive Future.
The future is sometimes used as a confident prediction, equivalent to an imperative.

Καὶ οὔποτε ἐρεῖ οὐδείς 1. 3. 5.
And no one shall ever say (= let no one ever say!).

153. Gnomic Future. — The future may be used, as in English, to express a general truth based on expectation.

Οὐδὲ ἄλλου οὐδενὸς ἐμψύχου κεφαλῆς γεύσεται Αἰγυπτίων οὐδείς Hdt. 2. 39.
Nor of any other animal's head does (will) any Egyptian taste.

154. Periphrastic Future with Μέλλω. — The future is expressed periphrastically by μέλλω with the infinitive, future, or present, rarely aorist (cf. 170, 242, 245, 247).

Ὁ ἐκ Βυζαντίου ἁρμοστὴς μέλλει ἥξειν 6. 4. 18.
The governor from Byzantium is about to come.

Μέλλομεν τούτους εἴργειν 3. 3. 16.
We are going (intend) to prevent them.

155. Periphrastic Future of the Past. — The imperfect of μέλλω with the infinitive may express a future of the past.

Πλησίον ἦν ὁ σταθμὸς ἔνθα ἔμελλε καταλύειν 1. 8. 1.
The halting place was near where he was to stop.

Οἱ πολέμιοι αὐτοὺς ὄψεσθαι ἔμελλον 4. 7. 16.
The enemy were about to see them.

THE FUTURE PERFECT TENSE

156. Action completed in Future Time. — The future perfect tense expresses an action as completed at some future time.

Οὕτως οἱ πολέμιοι πλεῖστον ἐψευσμένοι ἔσονται 3. 2. 31.
Thus the enemy will find themselves most deceived.

Πᾶς ὁ παρὼν φόβος λελύσεται Dem. 14. 2.
All the present fear will have been dispelled.

157. As Immediate Future. — The future perfect is sometimes used as an immediate future.

Ἡμῶν εὐθὺς Ἀριαῖος ἀφεστήξει· ὥστε φίλος ἡμῖν οὐδεὶς λελείψεται 2. 4. 5.
Ariaeus will at once withdraw from us; so that not a friend will be left us.

158. Future Perfect for Future.

Where the perfect has a present sense (cf. 138, 139), the future perfect is a simple future.

Οὐχ οὕτως ἐστήξει ὥσπερ πρόσθεν XC 6. 2. 17.
They (ἅρματα) will not stand as before.

Οἱ τύραννοι οὐδὲν ἀγαθὸν τοῦτο κεκτήσονται Pl. G. 467 a.
In this the tyrants will not possess any advantage.

THE TENSES OF THE OTHER MOODS

159. Not in Indirect Discourse.

The tenses of the subjunctive and imperative, and of the optative and infinitive not in indirect discourse, are the present, of continuance, the aorist, of attainment, and the perfect, of completion. The period of the action is determined by the context.

160. Subjunctive Present: Aorist.

Of the subjunctive mood the present and aorist tenses differ in general only as continuance differs from attainment; cf. the imperfect indicative: the aorist indicative (cf. 122).

Μὴ ἀναμένωμεν ἄλλους . . . ἀλλ' ἡμεῖς ἄρξωμεν 3. 1. 24.
Let us not wait for others, but ourselves begin.

Δοκεῖ μοι κατακαῦσαι τὰς ἁμάξας, . . . ἵνα μὴ τὰ ζεύγη ἡμῶν στρατηγῇ, ἀλλὰ πορευώμεθα ὅπῃ ἂν τῇ στρατιᾷ συμφέρῃ 3. 2. 27.
I think we should burn the wagons, in order that our baggage animals may not be our generals, but that we may proceed wherever it is best for the army.

Μὴ ὥσπερ οἱ λωτοφάγοι ἐπιλαθώμεθα τῆς οἰκάδε ὁδοῦ 3. 2. 25.
Lest, like the lotus-eaters, we forget our way home.

161. Aorist Subjunctive in Temporal Clauses.

But the aorist subjunctive in temporal clauses (cf. 222), after ἐπήν, ἐπειδάν, etc., *when, after*, etc., is regularly prior to the time of the leading verb.

Ἐπειδὰν διαπράξωμαι ἃ δέομαι, ἥξω 2. 3. 29.
When I shall have accomplished what I wish, I will come back.

Ἐπειδὰν ἅπαντα ἀκούσητε, κρίνατε, μὴ πρότερον προλαμβάνετε Dem. 4. 14.
When you have heard all, decide; do not prejudge.

Περιμένετε ἔστ' ἂν ἐγὼ ἔλθω 5. 1. 4.
Wait till I (have) come.

162. Perfect Subjunctive. — The perfect subjunctive expresses completed action.

Δέδοικα μή τινα λήθην ὑμῖν πεποιήκῃ Dem. 19. 3.
I fear lest it may have caused some forgetfulness in you.

163. Optative Present : Aorist. — Of the optative mood (not in indirect discourse) the present and aorist tenses differ in general only as continuance differs from attainment; cf. the imperfect indicative : the aorist indicative (cf. 122).

Οὐδὲ γὰρ ἂν Μήδοκός με . . . ἐπαινοίη, εἰ ἐξελαύνοιμι τοὺς εὐεργέτας 7. 7. 11.
For Medocus would not praise me, if I should banish my benefactors.

Οὐδ' εἰ πάντες ἔλθοιεν Πέρσαι, πλήθει γε οὐχ ὑπερβαλοίμεθ' ἂν τοὺς πολεμίους XC 2. 1. 8.
Not even if all the Persians should come, would we surpass the enemy in numbers.

164. Aorist Optative in Temporal Clauses. — But the aorist optative in temporal clauses (cf. 234), after ἐπεί, ἐπειδή, etc., *when, after*, etc., is regularly prior to the time of the leading verb (cf. 161).

Οὓς μὲν ἴδοι εὐτάκτως . . . ἰόντας, τίνες τε εἶεν ἠρώτα, καὶ ἐπεὶ πύθοιτο ἐπῄνει XC 5. 3. 55.
He asked those whom he saw marching in good order who they were, and when he had found out he praised them.

165. Perfect Optative. — The perfect optative expresses completed action.

Ἔδεισαν δὲ μὴ λύττα τις ὥσπερ κυσὶν ἡμῖν ἐμπεπτώκοι 5. 7. 26.
And they feared lest upon us, as upon dogs, some madness might have fallen.

166. Imperative Present : Aorist. — Of the imperative mood the present and aorist tenses differ in general only as continuance differs from attainment; cf. the imperfect indicative : the aorist indicative (cf. 122).

Ἀλλὰ διαλέγου καὶ μάθε πρῶτον τίνες εἰσίν 4. 8. 5.
But talk with them and find out first who they are.

Παρ' ἡμῶν δὲ ἀπάγγελλε τάδε 2. 1. 20.
But from us carry back the following reply.

Φάνητε τῶν λοχαγῶν ἄριστοι 3. 1. 24.
Show yourselves the best of captains.

Καὶ ὅτῳ δοκεῖ ταῦτ', ἔφη, ἀνατεινάτω τὴν χεῖρα 3. 2. 9.
And whoever approves of this, said he, let him raise his hand.

167. Subjunctive in Prohibitions. — In prohibitions, the aorist imperative is replaced as a rule (the second person always in prose) by the aorist subjunctive (212, 239). Thus λῦε : λῦσον : : μὴ λῦε : μὴ λύσῃς.

Μὴ ἐκδῶτέ με 6. 6. 17.
Do not give me over.

Cf. Τῷ μή μοι πατέρας ποθ' ὁμοίῃ ἔνθεο τιμῇ Δ 410.
Place not therefore our fathers in equal honor.

168. Perfect Imperative. — The perfect imperative, save from perfects used as presents, is rare. It denotes something decisive or final, and is commonest in the third person passive.

Ταῦτα μέν νυν περὶ τούτων εἰρήσθω Hdt. 6. 55.
Now let so much be said on this matter.

169. Infinitive Present : Aorist. — Of the infinitive mood (not in indirect discourse) the present and aorist tenses differ in general only as continuance differs from attainment; cf. the imperfect indicative : the aorist indicative (cf. 122).

Πολὺ γὰρ ῥᾷον ἔχοντας φυλάττειν ἢ κτήσασθαι πάντα πέφυκεν Dem. 2. 26.
For all things are far easier to keep, when we have them, than to get.

Ἐπιθυμῶν δὲ ἄρχειν 2. 6. 21.
Desiring to rule.

Βούλεται οὖν καὶ σὲ τούτων γεύσασθαι 1. 9. 26.
Therefore he wishes you also to taste them.

Μηχαναὶ πολλαί εἰσιν ὥστε διαφεύγειν θάνατον Pl. Ap. 39 a.
There are many devices to avoid death.

Ἔχω γὰρ τριήρεις ὥστε ἑλεῖν τὸ ἐκείνων πλοῖον 1. 4. 8.
For I have triremes (so as) to catch their boat.

170. Μέλλω with the Future Infinitive. — The future infinitive is used only in indirect discourse except after μέλλω (cf. 154, 245).

Θήσειν γὰρ ἔτ᾽ ἔμελλεν ἐπ᾽ ἄλγεά τε στοναχάς τε Β 39.
For he intended still to inflict upon them griefs and groans.

171. The Perfect Infinitive. — The perfect infinitive expresses completed action.

Οὐδὲ βουλεύεσθαι ἔτι ὥρα ἀλλὰ **βεβουλεῦσθαι** Pl. Cr. 46 a.
Nor is it any longer time to deliberate, but to be done with deliberation.

Εἴ πως δυναίμην φθάσαι πρὶν **κατειλῆφθαι** τὴν ὑπερβολήν 4. 1. 21.
If in any wise I might get there first before the pass had been occupied.

Οὓς ἢ ἀποκόψαι ἀνάγκη ἢ **διεζεῦχθαι** ἀπὸ τῶν ἄλλων Ἑλλήνων 4. 2. 10.
These they had to beat off or else be separated from the rest of the Greeks.

THE TENSES IN INDIRECT DISCOURSE

172. Correspondence of Tenses. — In indirect discourse (297 ff.) the tenses of the optative, the infinitive, and the participle stand as representatives of the corresponding tenses in the direct discourse, save that the imperfect and pluperfect indicative, if changed, become present and perfect respectively (cf. 306).

THE TENSES OF THE OPTATIVE

173. The Present Optative. — The present optative may represent the present indicative, subjunctive, optative, or (rarely) the imperfect indicative, of the direct discourse.

Ὑποψία μὲν ἦν ὅτι **ἄγοι** πρὸς βασιλέα 1. 3. 21 (O. R. ἄγει).
There was a suspicion that he was leading (them) against the king.

Ἐβουλεύετο . . . εἰ **πέμποιέν** τινας ἢ πάντες **ἴοιεν** 1. 10. 5 (O. R. πέμπωμεν ἢ ἴωμεν; cf. 213).
He took counsel whether they should send some or all should go.

Καὶ βασιλεῖ ἂν πολλοῦ ἄξιοι γένοιντο εἰ **βούλοιτο** φίλος γενέσθαι 2. 1. 14 (O. R. ἂν γενοίμεθα, βούλοιτο).
And they would prove valuable to the king if he would become their friend.

174. The Future Optative. — The future optative always represents the future indicative.

Ἔλεγεν ὅτι ἡ ὁδὸς **ἔσοιτο** πρὸς βασιλέα μέγαν 1. 4. 11 (O. R. ἔσται).
He said that the expedition was to be against the great king.

Γράφει ἐπιστολὴν παρὰ βασιλέα ὅτι **ἥξοι** 1. 6. 3 (O. R. ἥξω).
He wrote (a letter) to the king that he would come.

175. The Aorist Optative. — The aorist optative may represent the aorist indicative, subjunctive, or optative.

Λέγων ὅτι οὔπω δὴ πολλοῦ χρόνου τούτου ἡδίονι οἴνῳ **ἐπιτύχοι** 1. 9. 25.
Saying that he had not for a long time met with sweeter wine than this. (O. R. ἐπέτυχον.)

Ὑπισχνεῖτο, εἰ **διαβαῖεν**, μισθοφορὰν ἔσεσθαι τοῖς στρατιώταις 7. 1. 3.
He promised that, if they crossed, there would be pay for the soldiers. (O. R. ἐὰν διαβῆτε.)

For opt. in O. O. = opt. in O. R., cf. 2. 1. 14, § 173.

176. The Perfect Optative. — The perfect optative may represent the perfect indicative, subjunctive, or optative.

Ἡρώτησεν εἰ ἤδη **ἀποκεκριμένοι εἶεν** 2. 1. 15.
He asked if they had already replied. (O. R. ἀποκέκρισθε;)

177. The Future Perfect Optative. — The future perfect optative is very rare. It always represents the future perfect indicative.

TENSES OF THE INFINITIVE

178. The Present Infinitive. — The present infinitive may represent the present indicative, or optative, or the imperfect indicative.

Ἀδικεῖσθαι νομίζει 1. 3. 10.
He thinks he is wronged. (O. R. ἀδικοῦμαι.)

Ἔνιοι δὲ (φασίν), οὐδ' εἰ μεμνῇό τε καὶ βούλοιο, **δύνασθαι** ἂν ἀποδοῦναι 1. 7. 5.
And some (say) that, not even if you should remember, and wish to, could you pay. (O. R. δύναιτο ἄν.)

Καὶ **ἰᾶσθαι** αὐτὸς τὸ τραῦμά φησι 1. 8. 26.
And he says that he cured the wound himself. (O. R. αὐτὸς ἰώμην τὸ τραῦμα.)

179. The Future Infinitive. — The future infinitive represents only the future indicative.

Τὸν . . . στρατηγὸν προσδοκῶ ταῦτα **πράξειν** 3. 1. 14.
I expect the general will do this. (O. R. πράξει.)

180. The Aorist Infinitive. — The aorist infinitive may represent the aorist indicative or optative.

Μισθωθῆναι δὲ οὐκ ἐπὶ τούτῳ ἔφασαν 1. 3. 1.
And they said they had not been hired for this. (O. R. ἐμισθώθημεν.)

Ἐπίστευε μηδὲν ἂν παρὰ τὰς σπονδὰς **παθεῖν** 1. 9. 8.
He trusted that he would suffer nothing contrary to the truce. (O.R. οὐδὲν ἂν πάθοιμι.)

181. The Perfect Infinitive. — The perfect infinitive may represent the perfect indicative, or optative, or the pluperfect indicative.

Ὁμολογεῖς οὖν περὶ ἐμὲ ἄδικος **γεγενῆσθαι**; 1. 6. 8.
Do you then admit having been unjust toward me? (O. R. γεγένημαι.)

182. The Future Perfect Infinitive. — The future perfect infinitive represents only the future perfect indicative.

Οὐ **μεμνήσεσθαί** σέ φασιν 1. 7. 5.
They say you will not remember. (O. R. οὐ μεμνήσεται.)

The Participle

TENSES IN INDIRECT DISCOURSE

183. The Present Participle. — The present participle may represent the present indicative, or optative, or the imperfect indicative.

Αὐτῷ Κῦρον ... ἐπιστρατεύοντα πρῶτος ἤγγειλα 2. 3. 19.
I was the first to announce that Cyrus was marching against him.
(O. R. ἐπιστρατεύει.)

Οἶδα δὲ καὶ Σωκράτη δεικνύντα τοῖς συνοῦσιν ἑαυτὸν καλὸν κἀγαθὸν ὄντα
XM 1. 2. 18.
And I know that Socrates also showed to his associates that he was a good and noble man. (O. R. ἐδείκνυ.)

184. The Future Participle. — The future participle always represents the future indicative.

Ἀγνοεῖ τὸν ἐκεῖθεν πόλεμον δεῦρο ἥξοντα. Dem. 1. 15.
He does not know that the war in that quarter will come here.
(O. R. ἥξει.)

185. The Aorist Participle. — The aorist participle may represent the aorist indicative or optative.

Ἅπερ πολλοὺς καὶ ὑμεῖς ἴστε παθόντας 5. 8. 15.
Which very things you also know that many suffered. (O. R. ἔπαθον.)

Ὡς οὕτως περιγενόμενος ἂν τῶν ἀντιστασιωτῶν 1. 1. 10.
On the ground that he could thus get the better of his opponents.
(O. R. περιγενοίμην ἄν.)

186. The Perfect Participle. — The perfect participle may represent the perfect indicative or optative, or the pluperfect indicative.

Οὐ γὰρ ᾔδεσαν αὐτὸν τεθνηκότα 1. 10. 16.
For they did not know that he was dead. (O. R. τέθνηκε.)

187. The Future Perfect Participle. — The future perfect participle always represents the future perfect indicative.

TENSES NOT IN INDIRECT DISCOURSE

188. Relative Time. — The participle has, absolutely, no time of itself. Its tenses, not in indirect discourse, express time present, past, or future, relatively to that of the leading verb.

189. The Present Participle.
The present participle is regularly used of an action contemporaneous with that of the leading verb.

Κῦρος δὲ ψιλὴν ἔχων τὴν κεφαλὴν εἰς τὴν μάχην καθίστατο 1. 8. 6.
Cyrus went into the battle with his head bare.

Σύγε οὐδὲ ὁρῶν γιγνώσκεις οὐδὲ ἀκούων μέμνησαι 3. 1. 27.
As for you, not even when you see do you understand, nor when you hear do you remember.

190. The Present as an Imperfect Participle.
When the context makes it plain, the time of the present participle may be prior to that of the leading verb.

Οἱ Κύρειοι πρόσθεν σὺν ἡμῖν ταττόμενοι νῦν ἀφεστήκασιν 3. 2. 17.
The troops of Cyrus that were formerly marshaled with us have now deserted us.

Ἡ Πύλος . . . ἔστιν ἐν τῇ Μεσσηνίᾳ ποτὲ οὔσῃ γῇ Th. 4. 3.
Pylos is in the land that was once Messenia.

191. The Present Participle for Future.
With verbs of *going* or *sending* the present participle is sometimes used where we should expect a future, being logically subsequent in time to the leading verb.

Πρέσβεις πέμπειν ἐς Συρακούσας κωλύοντας μὴ ξυμβαίνειν Ἀθηναίοις Th. 6. 88. 10.
To send ambassadors to Syracuse to prevent their making terms with the Athenians.

192. The Future Participle.
The future participle is used of an action subsequent to that of the leading verb.

Λαγὼς ᾤχετο θηράσων 4. 5. 24.
He had gone off to hunt hares.

Ἦλθε . . . λυσόμενός τε θύγατρα A 12.
He came to ransom his daughter.

193. The Aorist Participle.
The aorist participle is regularly used of an action prior to that of the leading verb.

Ὁ δὲ λαβὼν τὸ χρυσίον στράτευμα συνέλεξεν I. 1. 9.
And he took the money and collected an army.

Ἀκούσαντες δ' οἱ στρατιῶται ἐχαλέπαινον I. 5. 11.
And, on hearing (him), the soldiers were angry.

194. The Aorist Participle for Present. — The aorist participle is sometimes used of action contemporaneous with that of the leading verb, especially when the latter is an aorist (cf. 275).

Καλῶς, ἔφη, ἐποίησας προειπών XC 1. 4. 13.
You have done well, said he, in forewarning me.

195. The Perfect Participle. — The perfect participle is used of action completed at the time of the leading verb.

Οὗτος δὲ τεταγμένος ἐτύγχανεν ἐπὶ τῷ εὐωνύμῳ I. 9. 31.
And he, as it chanced, had been stationed on the left.

Καὶ ἐπειρᾶτο κατάγειν τοὺς ἐκπεπτωκότας I. 1. 7.
And he tried to restore the exiles (those who had been banished).

196. The Future Perfect Participle. — The true future perfect participle is used of an action completed at a time subsequent to that of the leading verb. It is, however, little used, save as a simple future from verbs whose perfects have a present sense.

The Moods

THE INDICATIVE

197. In Independent Sentences. — The indicative, the mood of reality, is used in independent sentences much as in English.

Ῥεῖ ποταμός I. 2. 23.
A river flows.

Σὺν ὑμῖν ἕψομαι I. 3. 6.
I will follow with you.

Ἔχων οὓς εἴρηκα I. 2. 5.
With those whom I have mentioned.

Δύναμιν ἤθροιζεν I. 1. 6.
He was collecting a force.

Ἐνταῦθ' ἔμεινεν I. 2. 11.
There he remained.

Τί κατάκειμαι; 3. 1. 13.
Why do I lie here?

Σπονδὰς ἢ πόλεμον ἀπαγγελῶ; 2. 1. 23.
Shall I report a truce or war?

198. In Relative Clauses. — The indicative stands in relative clauses, except those that express general or future conditions (cf. 221, 233), or are future potential (cf. 226).

Συνέπεμψεν αὐτῇ στρατιώτας οὓς Μένων εἶχε 1. 2. 20.
He sent with her the soldiers whom Menon had.
Δῶρα ἃ νομίζεται παρὰ βασιλεῖ τίμια 1. 2. 27.
Gifts, such as are esteemed at court.

199. In Temporal Clauses. — The indicative stands in temporal clauses, unless they are conditional (cf. 222, 234).

Ἐπεὶ εἰσήλασεν εἰς τὴν πόλιν, μετεπέμπετο τὸν Συέννεσιν 1. 2. 26.
When he had entered the city, he sent for Syennesis.
Ἡνίκα δὲ δείλη ἐγίγνετο, ἐφάνη κονιορτός 1. 8. 8.
And when it was getting late, there was seen a cloud of dust.
Ἕως μὲν βάσιμα ἦν, ἐπὶ τοῦ ἵππου ἦγεν, ἐπεὶ δὲ ἄβατα ἦν, καταλιπὼν τὸν ἵππον ἔσπευδε πεζῇ 3. 4. 49.
As long as the road was passable, he led the way on horseback, but when it was impassable, he left his horse behind, and hastened on foot.

200. In Causal Clauses. — The indicative stands in causal clauses (cf. 237), after ὅτι, *because*, ἐπεί, ἐπειδή, *since;* also with εἰ, *if, that,* after verbs of emotion (*wonder,* etc.).

Ἡιτιᾶτο αὐτὸν ὅτι οὐχ ὑπέμεινεν 4. 1. 19.
He blamed him because he had not waited.
Ἐπεὶ ὑμεῖς ἐμοὶ οὐκ ἐθέλετε πείθεσθαι . . ., ἐγὼ σὺν ὑμῖν ἕψομαι 1. 3. 6.
Since you are not willing to obey me, I will follow with you.
Θαυμάζω δ' ἔγωγε εἰ μηδεὶς ὑμῶν μήτ' ἐνθυμεῖται μήτ' ὀργίζεται Dem. 4. 43.
But I for my part am surprised that no one of you is either concerned or angry.

201. In Indirect Discourse, Object Clauses. — The indicative stands in primary sequence of indirect discourse (cf. 293, 296) in object clauses introduced by the declarative conjunctions ὅτι or ὡς, *that*.

Λέγουσιν ὅτι βασιλεὺς κελεύει 2. 1. 8.
They say that the king commands.
Διδάσκειν σε βούλομαι ὡς σὺ ἡμῖν οὐκ ὀρθῶς ἀπιστεῖς 2. 5. 6.
I wish to show you that you are not right in distrusting us.

202. In Consecutive Clauses. — The indicative stands in clauses of actual result (cf. 252, 374) after ὥστε, *so that*, and in relative clauses of result.

Ὥστε βασιλεὺς τὴν μὲν πρὸς ἑαυτὸν ἐπιβουλὴν οὐκ ᾐσθάνετο 1. 1. 8.
So that the king did not perceive the plot against him.
Ὥστε καὶ μεταπεμπομένου αὐτοῦ οὐκ ἐθέλω ἐλθεῖν 1. 3. 10.
So that even though he keeps sending for me, I am not willing to go.
Τίς οὕτω μαίνεται ὅστις οὐ βούλεταί σοι φίλος εἶναι 2. 5. 12.
Who is so mad as not to wish to be your friend?

203. In Certain Conditional Clauses. — The indicative stands in present or past particular conditions after εἰ, *if* (cf. 314).

Εἰ μή τι κωλύει, ἐθέλω αὐτοῖς διαλεχθῆναι 4. 8. 4.
Unless something prevents, I wish to talk with them.
Εἴπερ ἐμοὶ ἐτέλει τι Σεύθης, οὐχ οὕτως ἐτέλει 7. 6. 16.
If indeed Seuthes paid me anything, he did not pay it thus.

Special Uses of the Future

204. In Object Clauses after Verbs of Effort. — The future indicative is regularly used (cf. 219, 231, 236) in object clauses with ὅπως, ὅπως μή, after verbs of effort, signifying *to strive, plan, take care*, etc. The leading verb may be omitted, and the clause has then the force of an exhortation or prohibition.

Βουλεύεται ὅπως μήποτε ἔτι ἔσται ἐπὶ τῷ ἀδελφῷ 1. 1. 4.
He plans never again to be in his brother's power.

Ὅπως δὲ καὶ ὑμεῖς ἐμὲ ἐπαινέσετε ἐμοὶ μελήσει 1. 4. 16.
And I shall take care that you also shall praise me.
Ὅπως οὖν ἔσεσθε ἄνδρες ἄξιοι τῆς ἐλευθερίας ἧς κέκτησθε 1. 7. 3.
See then that ye be men worthy of the freedom ye possess.

205. In Final Clauses. — The future indicative is used in relative clauses expressing purpose. It also occurs rarely with ὅπως, ὅπως μή, μή, in final clauses and after verbs of fear instead of the subjunctive (cf. 217).

Ἡγεμόνα αἰτεῖν Κῦρον ὅστις διὰ φιλίας τῆς χώρας ἀπάξει 1. 3. 14.
To ask Cyrus for a guide to lead them back through a friendly country.

Δέδοικα, ἔφη, μὴ ἄλλου τινὸς μᾶλλον ἢ τοῦ ἀγαθοῦ μεθέξω XC 2. 3. 6.
I fear, said he, that I shall share in something else rather than the good.

206. In a Future Condition. — The future indicative may stand in the protasis of a more vivid future condition, generally with a tone of threat or warning (cf. 316).

Εἰ γὰρ διατρίψομεν τὴν τήμερον ἡμέραν, οἱ . . . πολέμιοι θαρραλεώτεροι ἔσονται 4. 6. 9.
For if we delay to-day, the enemy will be bolder.

Special Uses of the Past Tenses

207. In Unreal Conditions. — The past tenses of the indicative are used in unreal conditions and in past potential clauses (cf. 320, 321, 327).

Εἰ τοῦτο πάντες ἐποιοῦμεν, ἅπαντες ἂν ἀπωλόμεθα 5. 8. 13.
If we all had done this, we should all have perished.

Ὑπό κεν ταλασίφρονά περ δέος εἷλεν Δ 421.
Fear might have seized even upon a man of stout heart.

208. In Hopeless Wishes. — The past tenses of the indicative are used in hopeless wishes (cf. 223) with εἴθε, εἰ γάρ, the imperfect in a wish that would alter the present, the aorist in a wish that would alter the past. This is a post-Homeric construction.

Εἴθε σοι, ὦ Περίκλεις, τότε συνεγενόμην XM 1. 2. 46.
Would that I then, O Pericles, had met thee!

209. Wishes with Ὤφελον. — The aorist ὤφελον, or εἰ γὰρ ὤφελον (in Homer αἰ γάρ, αἴθε), is frequently used to express a hopeless wish.

Ὤφελε μὲν Κῦρος ζῆν 2. 1. 4.
Would that Cyrus were alive.

Αἴθ᾽ ὄφελες παρὰ νηυσὶν ἀδάκρυτος καὶ ἀπήμων | ἧσθαι A 415.
Would thou wert sitting tearless and unharmed by the ships.

210. In an Unattainable Purpose. — The past tenses of the indicative are used with ἵνα or ὡς in clauses of unattainable purpose depending on some expression of non-reality (cf. 208, 320, 321).

Ἀλλὰ σὲ ἐχρῆν συγχωρεῖν, ἵνα συνουσία ἐγίγνετο Pl. Prot. 335 c.
But you should have yielded to us in order that our conversation might continue.

Ἔδει τὰ ἐνέχυρα τότε λαβεῖν, ὡς μηδ᾽ εἰ ἐβούλετο ἐδύνατο ἐξαπατᾶν 7. 6. 23.
You should then have exacted pledges so that he could not have deceived you even if he would.

THE SUBJUNCTIVE
In Independent Sentences

211. The Hortatory Subjunctive. — The subjunctive, chiefly of the first person, is used in exhortations and the like.

Ἴωμεν ἐπὶ τοὺς ἄνδρας 6. 5. 21.
Let us march against the men.

Μὴ πρὸς θεῶν μαινώμεθα, μηδ᾽ αἰσχρῶς ἀπολώμεθα 7. 1. 29.
Let us not, by the gods, be mad, nor ignobly perish.

212. Imperative Subjunctive. — The aorist subjunctive, chiefly of the second person, is used instead of the imperative in prohibitions (cf. 167, 239).

Μὴ ποιήσῃς ταῦτα 7. 1. 8.
Do not do this.

Μηδὲν ἀθυμήσητε ἕνεκα τῶν γεγενημένων 5. 4. 19.
Do not be at all discouraged on account of what has happened.

213. Deliberative Subjunctive. — The subjunctive, chiefly of the first person, is used in questions of appeal, nearly equivalent to a future indicative. It is sometimes preceded by βούλει or βούλεσθε without a connective.

Μηδ᾽ ἀποκρίνωμαι οὖν; XM 1. 2. 36.
Then I am not even to reply?

Δέξεσθε συμπότην ἢ ἀπίωμεν; Pl. Sym. 212 e.
Will you receive a fellow-reveler, or are we to go away?

Βούλει σοι εἴπω; Pl. G. 521 d.
Do you wish me to tell you?

214. Of Hesitating Statement. — The subjunctive is used, especially in Plato, in hesitating statements after μή and μὴ οὐ, as if a verb of fearing were understood (cf. 218).

Ἀλλὰ μὴ οὐ τοῦτ᾽ ᾖ χαλεπόν, ὦ ἄνδρες Ἀθηναῖοι, θάνατον ἐκφυγεῖν
Pl. Ap. 39 a.
But this is not, I suspect, a hard thing, men of Athens, to escape death.

215. Aorist Subjunctive with Οὐ μή. — Οὐ μή with the aorist subjunctive is equivalent to an emphatic future. The future indicative may also be used (cf. 343).

Τὰ μὲν γὰρ ξένια οὐ μὴ γένηται τῇ στρατιᾷ τριῶν ἡμερῶν σῖτα 6. 2. 4.
For the hospitable gifts will not provision the army for three days.

Οὐδεὶς μηκέτι μείνῃ (*v.l.* μενεῖ) τῶν πολεμίων 4. 8. 13.
None of the enemy will remain any longer.

216. Homeric Subjunctive as Future. — In Homer the subjunctive, with or without ἄν (κέ), is used freely as a future tense (cf. 227).

Οὐ γάρ πω τοίους ἴδον ἀνέρας, οὐδὲ ἴδωμαι A 262.
For I never yet saw, nor shall I see such men.

Ἐγὼ δέ κ' ἄγω Βρισηίδα καλλιπάρῃον A 184.
And I shall fetch the fair-cheeked Briseis.

In Dependent Clauses

217. In Final Clauses. — The subjunctive stands in final clauses after ἵνα, ὡς, ὅπως, μή (ὄφρα poetical), in primary sequence (cf. 205, 229).

Κατάμενε ἵνα καὶ περὶ σοῦ βουλευσώμεθα 6. 6. 28.
Wait here that we may deliberate concerning you also.

Πάντα ποιητέα ὡς μήποτ' ἐπὶ τοῖς βαρβάροις γενώμεθα 3. 1. 35.
Every means must be used that we may never fall into the power of the barbarians.

Ὅπως δὲ καὶ εἰδῆτε εἰς οἷον ἔρχεσθε ἀγῶνα, ὑμᾶς εἰδὼς διδάξω 1. 7. 4.
And that you also may know what sort of a contest you are entering, I, who know, will inform you.

Κεφαλῇ κατανεύσομαι ὄφρα πεποίθῃς A 524.
I will nod with my head that you may trust me.

218. After Verbs of Fear. — The subjunctive stands after μή, μὴ οὐ, with verbs of fear in primary sequence (cf. 230, 338).

Δεδιὼς μὴ λαβών με δίκην ἐπιθῇ 1. 3. 10.
Fearing lest he may seize and inflict punishment on me.

Οὐ τοῦτο δέδοικα, μὴ οὐκ ἔχω ὅ τι δῶ (cf. 213) ἑκάστῳ τῶν φίλων 1. 7. 7.
I am not afraid of this, that I shall not have enough to give to each of my friends.

219. In Object Clauses with Ὅπως. — Verbs of effort (*to strive, plan*, etc.) sometimes take the subjunctive with ὅπως, or ὅπως ἄν, in primary sequence instead of the future indicative (cf. 204, 231, 236).

Πειρᾶσθαι ὅπως, ἢν μὲν δυνώμεθα, καλῶς νικῶντες σῳζώμεθα 3. 2. 3.
To strive that if possible we may conquer nobly and be saved.

Τῶν ἄλλων ἐπιμέλεται ὅπως ἂν θηρῶσιν XC 1. 2. 10.
He takes care that the others may hunt.

220. In Conditions. — The subjunctive is used in conditions after ἐάν (ἤν, ἄν), *if* (315, 323).

Ἐάν τέ τις πιέζηται τῶν λόχων, ὁ πλησίον βοηθήσει 4. 8. 13.
And if one of the companies be hard pressed, the next one will help.
Ἂν δὲ πλέητε, ἔστιν ἐνθένδε μὲν εἰς Σινώπην παραπλεῦσαι 5. 6. 10.
But if you go by ship, you can sail along from here to Sinope.

221. In Conditional Relative Clauses. — The subjunctive is used in conditional relative clauses after ὃς ἄν, ὅστις ἄν, etc. (cf. 233).

Καὶ σὺν ὑμῖν ὅ τι ἂν δέῃ πείσομαι 1. 3. 5.
And with you I will suffer whatever may be necessary.
Ἡγεῖται τοῦ στρατεύματος ὁποῖον ἂν ἀεὶ πρὸς τὴν χώραν συμφέρῃ 7. 3. 37.
That part of the army leads whichever from time to time is suited to the ground.

222. In Conditional Temporal Clauses. — The subjunctive is used in conditional temporal (local, and modal, cf. 375) clauses after ὅταν, ἐπειδάν, ἕως ἄν, πρὶν ἄν, etc. (cf. 234, 373).

Ἕως μὲν ἂν παρῇ τις, χρῶμαι, ἐπειδὰν δὲ ἀπιέναι βούληται, ... αὐτοὺς κακῶς ποιῶ 1. 4. 8.
As long as any one stays by me, I make use of him, but when he desires to go away, I injure him (them).
Ὑμᾶς, ἐπειδὰν ἐκεῖσε ἥκητε, δεξόμεθα ὡς ἂν δυνώμεθα κάλλιστα 6. 6. 36.
When you come there, we shall receive you as well as we can.

THE OPTATIVE
In Independent Sentences

223. The Optative of Wish. — The optative is used to express a future wish (cf. 208), with or without εἴθε, εἰ γάρ (poetic αἴθε, αἰ γάρ).

Τούτους μὲν οἱ θεοὶ ἀποτείσαιντο 3. 2. 6.
These men may the gods requite!

§ 227] OPTATIVE MOOD 65

Πολλά μοι κἀγαθὰ γένοιτο 5. 6. 4.   Αἲ γὰρ δὴ οὕτως εἴη Δ 189.
May many good things be mine!   O that this may be so!

224. Imperative Optative. — The optative of wish sometimes has almost the force of a command.

Μήτε πολεμεῖτε Λακεδαιμονίοις σῳζοισθέ τε 6. 6. 18.
War not with the Lacedaemonians, but be saved!

Εἰ μὲν οὖν ἄλλο τις βέλτιον ὁρᾷ, ἄλλως ἐχέτω· εἰ δὲ μή, Χειρίσοφος μὲν ἡγοῖτο 3. 2. 37.
Now if any one has another (and a) better plan, let it be otherwise; but if not, let Chirisophus lead.

225. The Apodosis Optative. — The optative with ἄν (κέ) is used in the apodosis of a less vivid future condition (317).

Πορευοίμεθα δ' ἂν οἴκαδε, εἴ τις ἡμᾶς μὴ λυποίη 2. 3. 23.
We would march home, if no one should molest us.

Ἀλλ' εἴ μοί τι πίθοιο, τό κεν πολὺ κέρδιον εἴη Η 28.
But if you would at all obey me, that would be far better.

226. The Potential Optative. — The optative with ἄν (κέ) is used in a future potential sense, with no condition implied.

Ἔνθα πολλὴν μὲν σωφροσύνην **καταμάθοι** ἄν τις 1. 9. 3.
There one may learn much self-control.

Πρόσθεν ἂν **ἀποθάνοιεν** ἢ τὰ ὅπλα **παραδοῖεν** 2. 1. 10.
They would sooner die than surrender their arms.

Μυσούς, οὓς οὐκ ἂν ἡμῶν **φαίημεν** βελτίους εἶναι 3. 2. 23.
The Mysians, whom we should not call our superiors.

227. Homeric Optative as Future. — In Homer the optative with ἄν, or κέ (rarely without ἄν, or κέ), is used as a future tense, nearly or quite equivalent to a future indicative (cf. 216).

Τῷ δέ κε νικήσαντι γυνὴ καὶ κτήματ' ἕποιτο· | οἱ δ' ἄλλοι φιλότητα καὶ ὅρκια πιστὰ ταμόντες | **ναίοιμεν** Τροίην ἐριβώλακα Γ 255.
And the woman and her goods shall go with the victor; but the rest of us, having pledged friendship and faithful oaths, shall dwell in fertile Troy.

In Dependent Clauses

228. Optative and Subjunctive. — In dependent clauses the optative, save in indirect discourse (297 ff.), corresponds to the subjunctive as secondary to primary, *i.e.* it follows secondary tenses in the same constructions in which the subjunctive follows primary tenses (cf. 294, 295).

Λέξον, ἵνα οὗτοι ἀπαγγέλλωσιν 7. 2. 35.
Speak, that these may report.

Δῆλος ἦν . . . ἐπιθυμῶν δὲ τιμᾶσθαι, ἵνα πλείω κερδαίνοι 2. 6. 21.
And he was evidently desirous of being honored, that he might make larger gains.

229. In Final Clauses. — The optative stands in final clauses after ἵνα, ὡς, ὅπως, μή, (ὄφρα), in secondary sequence (cf. 217).

Φίλος ἐβούλετο εἶναι τοῖς μέγιστα δυναμένοις, ἵνα ἀδικῶν μὴ διδοίη δίκην 2. 6. 21.
He wished to be a friend to those who were most powerful in order that he might not pay the penalty of his wrongdoing.

Ἠνάγκασα δὲ σὲ τοῦτον ἄγειν ὡς μὴ ἀπόλοιτο 5. 8. 8.
And I forced you to carry him that he might not perish.

Ἐκάλεσε γάρ τις αὐτὸν τῶν ὑπηρετῶν ὅπως ἴδοι 2. 1. 9.
For one of his servants called him that he might see.

230. After Verbs of Fear. — The optative stands after μή, μὴ οὐ, with verbs of fear, in secondary sequence (cf. 218, 338).

Ἐφοβοῦντο μὴ ἐπιθοῖντο αὐτοῖς 3. 4. 1.
They feared lest they might attack them.

Ἐφοβεῖτο . . . μὴ οὐ δύναιτο ἐκ τῆς χώρας ἐξελθεῖν 3. 1. 12.
He feared that he would not be able to go out of the country.

231. In Object Clauses with Ὅπως. — Verbs of effort (*to strive, plan*, etc.) sometimes take the optative with ὅπως, in secondary sequence, instead of the future indicative (cf. 204, 219, 236).

Ἐκέλευε διαπρᾶξαι ὅπως εἰς τὸ τεῖχος εἰσέλθοι 7. 1. 38.
He bade him manage to enter within the wall.

Ἀπεκρίνατο ὅτι αὐτῷ μέλοι ὅπως καλῶς ἔχοι 1. 8. 13.
He replied that he was taking care that all should be well.

232. In Conditions. — The optative is used in less vivid future and past general conditions after εἰ, *if* (317, 324).

Ἂν ἐλπίδων ἐμαυτὸν στερήσαιμι, εἰ σέ τι κακὸν ἐπιχειρήσαιμι ποιεῖν 2. 5. 10.
I should deprive myself of hope, if I should attempt to wrong you in anything.

Οὐκ ἀπελείπετο ἔτι αὐτοῦ, εἰ μή τι ἀναγκαῖον εἴη XM 4. 2. 40.
He left him no more, unless there was some necessity for it.

233. In Conditional Relative Clauses. — The optative is used in conditional relative clauses after ὅς, ὅστις, etc., in secondary sequence (cf. 221).

Ὁπόσα λαμβάνοι πλοῖα κατῆγεν 5. 1. 16.
Whatever vessels he took, he brought to land.

Ἐγὼ γὰρ ὀκνοίην μὲν ἂν εἰς τὰ πλοῖα ἐμβαίνειν ἃ ἡμῖν δοίη 1. 3. 17.
For I should hesitate to embark on the vessels which he might give us.

234. In Conditional Temporal Clauses. — The optative is used in conditional temporal (local, and modal, cf. 375) clauses after ὅτε, ἐπειδή, ἕως, πρίν, etc., in secondary sequence (cf. 222).

Καὶ οἱ μὲν ὄνοι, ἐπεί τις διώκοι, προδραμόντες ἔστασαν 1. 5. 2.
And the asses, when any one chased them, ran on ahead and stopped.

Ὅπου μὲν στρατηγὸς σῶς εἴη, τὸν στρατηγὸν παρεκάλουν 3. 1. 32.
Where a general was safe, they called the general.

235. In Indirect Discourse. — The optative stands in indirect discourse after ὅτι or ὡς, and in indirect questions, in secondary sequence (cf. 296).

Ἔλεγεν ὅτι ἡ ὁδὸς ἔσοιτο πρὸς βασιλέα μέγαν 1. 4. 11.
He said that the march was to be against the great king (O. R. ἔσται).

Ὅ τι δὲ ποιήσοι οὐ διεσήμηνε 2. 1. 23.
But what he would do he did not declare (O. R. τί ποιήσεις ;).

236. In Implied Indirect Discourse, Object Clauses. — Verbs of effort (*to strive, plan*, etc.) may be followed by ὅπως and the future optative in secondary sequence, corresponding to ὅπως and the future indicative in primary sequence (cf. 204, 219, 231).

Ἐπεμελεῖτο δὲ ὅπως μήτε ἄσιτοι μήτε ἄποτοί ποτε ἔσοιντο XC 8. 1. 43.
And he took care that they should never be either without food or drink.

237. In Implied Indirect Discourse, Causal Clauses. — The optative may stand in secondary sequence in causal clauses (cf. 200) after ὅτι, *because*, ἐπεί, ἐπειδή, *since*, etc., when the reason is assigned on the authority of some one else than the author.

Ἐβόα ἄγειν τὸ στράτευμα κατὰ μέσον τὸ τῶν πολεμίων, ὅτι ἐκεῖ βασιλεὺς εἴη 1. 8. 12.
He called out to lead the army against the center of the enemy, because the king (*as he, not Xenophon, thought*) was there.

Ὁ δ' ἐχαλέπαινεν ὅτι . . . πρᾴως λέγοι τὸ αὑτοῦ πάθος 1. 5. 14.
And he was angry because he (Menon) spoke lightly of his experience.

238. The Optative by Assimilation. — The optative may stand in clauses depending upon other optatives, by assimilation.

Ἔδοξέ μοι εἰς λόγους σοι ἐλθεῖν, ὅπως, εἰ δυναίμεθα, ἐξέλοιμεν ἀλλήλων τὴν ἀπιστίαν 2. 5. 4.
I thought best to come into conference with you, in order that, if we could, we might free each other of our distrust.

Οὐκ ἄν, ὁπότε οἱ πολέμιοι ἔλθοιεν, βουλεύεσθαι ἡμᾶς δέοι 3. 2. 36.
We should not have to plan, when the enemy comes.

THE IMPERATIVE

239. Commands. — The imperative is the mood of command, but the aorist imperative is scarcely used at all in prohibitions (167, 212).

Ἀπάγγελλε τάδε 2. 1. 20.
Report as follows.

Μὴ θαυμάζετε 1. 3. 3.
Marvel not.

Ἡμῖν εἰπὲ τί λέγεις 2. 1. 15.
Tell us what you intend.

Cf. Μὴ ποιήσῃς ταῦτα 7. 1. 8.
Do not do this.

Ἀλλὰ ἰόντων 1. 4. 8.
But let them go.

Μηδεὶς ὑμῶν λεγέτω 1. 3. 15.
Let no one of you say.

Ἀνατεινάτω τὴν χεῖρα 3. 2. 9.
Let him raise his hand.

Cf. Μὴ ἐκδῶτέ με 6. 6. 17.
Do not give me over.

240. Imperative in Dependent Clauses. — The imperative is sometimes used in relative clauses, particularly after οἶσθ' ὅ, and after ἐπεί.

Ἀλλ' οἶσθ' ὃ δρᾶσον; τῷ σκέλει θένε τὴν πέτραν Ar. Av. 54.
But do you know what you must do? Strike the rock with your leg.

Λέγουσιν δὲ καὶ ἄλλους τινὰς ἄλλοι πόρους, ὧν ἕλεσθ' ὅστις ὑμῖν συμφέρειν δοκεῖ Dem. 1. 20.
And others mention certain other means, of which choose whichever seems to you advantageous.

241. Substitutes for Imperative. — A number of other forms may be used as substitutes for the imperative (cf. 212, 224, 256).

THE INFINITIVE

In Indirect Discourse

242. After Verbs of Thought and Expression. — The infinitive is used in indirect discourse depending on verbs of saying, believing, and thinking (298).

Ὁμολογεῖς οὖν περὶ ἐμὲ ἄδικος γεγενῆσθαι 1. 6. 8.
Do you then admit that you have been unjust to me? (O. R. γεγένημαι).

Οἴει τὴν ὑμετέραν ἀρετὴν **περιγενέσθαι** ἂν τῆς βασιλέως δυνάμεως 2. 1. 13.
You think that your valor would overcome the force of the king
(O. R. περιγένοιτο ἄν).

243. Historical Infinitive.
— In continuous narrative the verb of saying (*e.g.* λέγεται) is sometimes implied but not expressed. The infinitive then must be translated as a narrative tense of the indicative.

Καὶ τὸν Κῦρον ἀκούσαντα **κελεῦσαι** τοὺς ἑρμηνέας **ἐπείρεσθαι** τὸν Κροῖσον, τίνα τοῦτον ἐπικαλέοιτο Hdt. 1. 86.
And Cyrus, having heard him, bade the interpreters ask Croesus who this was on whom he called.

244. In Dependent Clauses by Assimilation.
— In indirect discourse the infinitive may stand by assimilation even in dependent clauses. This is commonest in relative and temporal clauses.

Εἶναι Πέρσας ἑαυτοῦ βελτίους, οὓς οὐκ ἂν **ἀνασχέσθαι** αὐτοῦ βασιλεύοντος
2. 2. 1.
(He said) there were Persians better than himself who would not endure him as king.

Ὡς δὲ ἄρα μιν **προστῆναι** τοῦτο . . . ἐς τρὶς ὀνομάσαι (243) Σόλωνα
Hdt. 1. 86.
And when this thought came to him, he thrice called on Solon.

245. After Verbs of Hoping, etc.
— Verbs of *hoping, promising, swearing*, and the like, generally take the future infinitive on the principle of indirect discourse (cf. 242), but they may also take a present or aorist complementary infinitive (cf. 247). Even φημί is occasionally thus used in Homer.

Ὁ δ' ὑπέσχετο ἀνδρὶ ἑκάστῳ **δώσειν** πέντε ἀργυρίου μνᾶς 1. 4. 13.
But he promised to give to each man five silver minae.

Ὀμόσαι ἦ μὴν **πορεύσεσθαι** ὡς διὰ φιλίας ἀσινῶς 2. 3. 27.
To swear, assuredly to march without doing damage, as if through a friendly country.

Cf. Προσαγαγὼν καὶ ἐγγυητὰς ἦ μὴν **πορεύεσθαι** XC 6. 2. 39.
Having given sureties also that he would certainly go.

Ἠπείλησαν ἀποκτεῖναι ἅπαντας ΧΗ 5. 4. 7.
They threatened to kill all.

Ἐφάμην τείσασθαι Ἀλέξανδρον Γ 366.
I expected to punish Alexander.

Not in Indirect Discourse

246. The Infinitive as Subject. — The infinitive may be used as subject, particularly with impersonal verbs or phrases.

Ἔδοξεν αὐτοῖς ἀπιέναι 1. 10. 17.
It seemed to them best to depart.

Παρῆν μετρεῖν τὸ βάθος τῆς χιόνος 4. 5. 6.
It was possible to measure the depth of the snow.

Φεύγειν αὐτοῖς ἀσφαλέστερόν ἐστιν 3. 2. 19.
It is safer for them to flee.

247. Complementary Infinitive. — The infinitive is used with many verbs whose action implies a supplementary action. It may stand to the leading verb in the relation of an accusative object or of a genitive object.

Ἐμελέτων τοξεύειν 3. 4. 17.
They practiced shooting.

Μανθάνουσιν ἄρχειν τε καὶ ἄρχεσθαι 1. 9. 4.
They learn how to rule and to be ruled.

Ἐβούλετο τὼ παῖδε ἀμφοτέρω παρεῖναι 1. 1. 1.
He wished both his sons to be with him.

Τὸ ὑπολειπόμενον ἤρξατο δρόμῳ θεῖν 1. 8. 18.
The part left behind began to go on a run.

248. Complementary Infinitive with Adjectives, etc. — The infinitive is used in dependence on many adjectives and nouns of *fitness, power, capacity*, etc.

Ἄρχειν ἀξιώτατος 1. 9. 1.
Most worthy to rule.

Τὰ μεγάλα πράττειν ἱκανός 2. 6. 16.
Capable of doing great things.

Ὥρα λέγειν 1. 3. 12.
Time to speak.

Κίνδυνος οὖν πολλοὺς ἀπόλλυσθαι 5. 1. 6.
There is danger therefore of **many** perishing.

249. Infinitive of Purpose.

The infinitive is used to express purpose (cf. 259), particularly after verbs of *choosing*, *giving*, etc.

Εἵλοντο δὲ Δρακόντιον . . . δρόμου . . . ἐπιμεληθῆναι 4. 8. 25.
And they chose Dracontius to take charge of the running.

Ταύτην τὴν χώραν ἐπέτρεψε διαρπάσαι τοῖς Ἕλλησιν 1. 2. 19.
This country he gave over to the Greeks to plunder.

Special Uses

250. After Comparatives and Ἤ.

The infinitive after the comparative with ἤ depends on the implied notion of ability. It may be introduced by ὥστε or ὡς (252).

Τὸ γὰρ νόσημα μεῖζον ἢ φέρειν Soph. OT 1293.
For the distress is too great to bear.

Ἡισθοντο αὐτὸν ἐλάττω ἔχοντα δύναμιν ἢ ὥστε τοὺς φίλους ὠφελεῖν
XH 4. 8. 23.
They perceived that he had too small a force to aid his friends.

251. After Πρίν.

After the comparative πρίν (poetic πάρος) Attic prose uses the infinitive without ἤ (cf. 199, 222, 234).

Πρὶν δῆλον εἶναι τί ποιήσουσιν 1. 4. 13.
Before it was clear what they would do.

Πρὶν δὲ ἀρίστου ὥραν εἶναι 6. 5. 1.
And before it was breakfast time.

Πάρος τάδε ἔργα γενέσθαι Z 348.
Before these deeds were done.

252. Infinitive of Result with Ὥστε.

The infinitive is used to express result or tendency, shading over into purpose, after ὥστε, or ὡς, *so as* (cf. 202, 374).

Ἐλαφροὶ γὰρ ἦσαν ὥστε καὶ ἐγγύθεν φεύγοντες ἀποφεύγειν 4. 2. 27.
For they were nimble enough (so as) to escape even when they fled from close quarters.

Ἔχω γὰρ τριήρεις ὥστε ἑλεῖν τὸ ἐκείνων πλοῖον 1. 4. 8.
For I have triremes (so as) to catch their boat.

Συνέσπων ὡς μὴ ἅπτεσθαι τῆς κάρφης τὸ ὕδωρ 1. 5. 10.
They sewed them up so that the water should not touch the hay.

253. After Ἐφ' ᾧ, Ἐφ' ᾧτε.
— In a similar way the infinitive is used with ἐφ' ᾧ, ἐφ' ᾧτε, *on condition that*.

Οἱ δ' ἔφασαν ἀποδώσειν ἐφ' ᾧ μὴ κάειν τὰς οἰκίας 4. 2. 19.
And they said they would give them up on condition that they should not burn the houses.

Ἐφ' ᾧτε πλοῖα συλλέγειν 6. 6. 22.
On condition (for the purpose) of collecting boats.

254. Epexegetical Infinitive.
— The infinitive may follow an adjective or noun to limit its meaning.

Ὁρᾶν στυγνὸς ἦν 2. 6. 9.
He was gloomy to look at.

Αἰεί τοι τὰ κάκ' ἐστὶ φίλα φρεσὶ μαντεύεσθαι A 107.
Always are evils pleasant to thy heart to predict.

Θαῦμα ἰδέσθαι Θ 366.
A marvel to behold.

255. Absolute Infinitive.
— The infinitive is used absolutely in many phrases, mostly parenthetical. Such are: —

Ὡς εἰπεῖν, ὡς ἔπος εἰπεῖν.   Ἐμοὶ δοκεῖν.
So to speak.   In my opinion.

Ὀλίγου δεῖν.   Ἑκὼν εἶναι.
Almost.   Voluntarily.

256. The Imperative Infinitive.
— The infinitive is used in an imperative sense, particularly in Homer and Herodotus.

Ἐπισχέειν, μηδὲ καλέειν κω ὄλβιον, ἀλλ' εὐτυχέα Hdt. 1. 33.
Wait, and call him not yet happy, but fortunate.

Παῖδα δ' ἐμοὶ λῦσαί τε φίλην, τά τ' ἄποινα δέχεσθαι A 20.
But release me my daughter, and accept this ransom.

257. The Exclamatory Infinitive.
— The infinitive is used absolutely in exclamations.

Τοῦτον δὲ ὑβρίζειν Dem. 21. 209.
And to think that he should be insolent!

The Articular Infinitive

258. As a Noun in Case Relations. — The infinitive with the article is used freely in all noun constructions, as subject, object, with prepositions, etc.

Τῶν γὰρ μάχῃ νικώντων καὶ τὸ ἄρχειν ἐστί 2. 1. 4.
For even the sovereignty belongs to the victors.

Τὸ μὲν διαρρίπτειν εἴα χαίρειν 7. 3. 23.
The distribution (of food) he let pass.

Ἄλλη πρόφασις ἦν αὐτῷ τοῦ ἀθροίζειν στράτευμα 1. 1. 7.
He had another pretext for collecting an army.

Ἠγάλλετο τῷ ἐξαπατᾶν δύνασθαι 2. 6. 26.
He gloried in the ability to deceive.

Τοῦτο δ' ἐποίει ἐκ τοῦ χαλεπὸς εἶναι 2. 6. 9.
And this he did from being harsh.

259. The Genitive of Purpose. — The genitive of the articular infinitive is used to express purpose (cf. 249), particularly in the orators.

Τοῦ μὴ τὰ δίκαια ποιεῖν Dem. 18. 107.
In order to escape doing what was just.

Τοῦ μηδένα ἔτι ἐξιέναι Th. 2. 75.
That no one might any more go forth.

260. The Genitive after Verbs of Hindering. — The genitive of the articular infinitive is used after verbs and expressions of *hindering*, etc., and may be accompanied by a redundant μή.

(Εἶπεν ὅτι ἂν) κωλύσειε τοῦ κάειν ἐπιόντας 1. 6. 2.
(He said that) he would prevent them from attacking and burning.

Πᾶς γὰρ ἀσκὸς δύο ἄνδρας ἕξει τοῦ μὴ καταδῦναι 3. 5. 11.
For every skin will keep two men from sinking.

261. The Adverbial Accusative. — The accusative of the articular infinitive is used freely in adverbial relation to a noun, adjective, or clause.

Τὸ μὲν ἐς τὴν γῆν ἡμῶν ἐσβάλλειν ... ἱκανοί εἰσι Th. 6. 17.
They are able to invade our land.

Τὸ κατὰ τοῦτον εἶναι 1. 6. 9.
As far as he is concerned.

The Participle

THE ATTRIBUTIVE PARTICIPLE

262. As a Verbal Adjective. — The attributive participle has the function of a verbal adjective. It is often best translated by a relative clause.

Οἱ παρόντες Ἕλληνες 1. 5. 16.　　Τὸ διαβαῖνον στράτευμα 4. 3. 24.
The Greeks who are present.　　The army that was crossing.

Ὁρῶσι δὲ τοὺς διαβαίνειν κωλύσοντας, ὁρῶσι δὲ τοῖς διαβαίνουσιν ἐπικεισομένους τοὺς Καρδούχους 4. 3. 7.
They see men ready to prevent their crossing, and they see the Carduchians ready to attack those who started to cross.

263. Potential Participle with ἄν. — The attributive participle with ἄν may be potential, or may represent an apodosis, just as the potential optative with ἄν (cf. 226) may stand in a relative clause.

Οὔτε ὄντα οὔτε ἂν γενόμενα λογοποιοῦσιν Th. 6. 38.
They invent tales that neither are (true) nor could come (true).

Σκέμματα ... τῶν ῥᾳδίως ἀποκτιννύντων καὶ ἀναβιωσκομένων γ᾽ ἄν, εἰ οἷοί τε ἦσαν Pl. Cr. 48 c.
Considerations of those who lightly slay, and would bring to life again, if they could.

264. Used Substantively. — The attributive participle, like any adjective, is often used substantively.

Τὰ παρόντα 3. 1. 34.　　Τὸ ὑπολειπόμενον 1. 8. 18.
The present circumstances.　　The part left behind.

Καὶ ἐπειρᾶτο κατάγειν τοὺς ἐκπεπτωκότας 1. 1. 7.
And he endeavored to restore the exiles.

265. Predicate Periphrases.

— The participle may be used in the predicate after εἰμί, practically as a periphrastic tense-form.

Ἦν δὲ αὕτη ἡ στρατηγία οὐδὲν ἄλλο δυναμένη ἢ ἀποδρᾶναι 2. 2. 13.
But this plan of campaign amounted to nothing else than flight.

Φιλοκίνδυνός τε ἦν καὶ ἡμέρας καὶ νυκτὸς ἄγων ἐπὶ τοὺς πολεμίους 2. 6. 7.
He was fond of danger, and by day and by night ready to lead against the enemy.

THE CIRCUMSTANTIAL PARTICIPLE

266. Sphere of the Circumstantial Participle.

— The participle may define the circumstances of an action, implying a variety of relations to the leading verb, such as *time, means, manner*, etc. It may agree with the subject or with some part of the predicate.

Ἀκούσας (w. subj.) δὲ ταῦτα ὁ Φαλῖνος ἐγέλασε 2. 1. 13.
And Phalinus, when he heard this, burst out laughing.

Παίοντα (w. obj.) δ' αὐτὸν ἀκοντίζει τις παλτῷ 1. 8. 27.
As he was striking, some one smites him with a javelin.

Ἀκούσασι τοῖς στρατηγοῖς ταῦτα ἔδοξε τὸ στράτευμα συναγαγεῖν 4. 4. 19.
When the generals heard this, they resolved to collect their army.

267. Of Time.

— The circumstantial participle may define the time of an action.

Πολὺν χρόνον διαλεχθέντες ἀλλήλοις ἀπῆλθον 2. 5. 42.
After a long conference with one another they departed.

Ταῦτα ποιήσαντες ἠριστοποιοῦντο 3. 3. 1.
When they had done this they breakfasted.

268. Of Means.

— The circumstantial participle may express the means of an action.

Κρέα οὖν ἐσθίοντες οἱ στρατιῶται διεγίγνοντο 1. 5. 6.
So the soldiers subsisted by eating flesh.

Οἷς πᾶσι χρώμενοι κρέα ἕψοντες ἤσθιον 2. 1. 6.
By using all these they cooked and ate their meat.

269. Of Manner.
The circumstantial participle may define the manner of an action.

Ἐπί τε τοῦ ἅρματος **καθήμενος** τὴν πορείαν ἐποιεῖτο καὶ ὀλίγους ἐν τάξει ἔχων πρὸ αὑτοῦ 1. 7. 20.

He made the march sitting on his chariot, and with but few in line before him.

Ἀπῆλθον οὐδὲν **ἀποκρινάμενοι** 2. 5. 42.

They went away without replying.

270. Of Cause.
The circumstantial participle may express the cause or ground of an action, often with ἅτε, οἷα, or οἷον (as the author's thought), or with ὡς (as another's thought).

Οἱ γὰρ Κόλχοι, ἅτε **ἐκπεπτωκότες** τῶν οἰκιῶν, πολλοὶ ἦσαν ἀθρόοι 5. 2. 1.

For the Colchians, since they had been expelled from their homes, were collected in large numbers.

Ἐθανατώθη ὑπὸ τῶν ἐν τῇ Σπάρτῃ τελῶν ὡς **ἀπειθῶν** 2. 6. 4.

He was condemned to death by the magistrates in Sparta on the ground of disobedience.

271. Of Purpose.
The circumstantial participle may express the purpose of an action. It is generally future, often accompanied by ὡς.

Ὁ δ' ἀνὴρ αὐτῆς λαγὼς ᾤχετο **θηράσων** 4. 5. 24.

But her husband had gone off to hunt hares.

Μὴ ἀναμένωμεν ἄλλους ἐφ' ἡμᾶς ἐλθεῖν **παρακαλοῦντας** ἐπὶ τὰ κάλλιστα ἔργα 3. 1. 24.

Let us not wait for others to come to us to encourage us to the noblest deeds.

Οὔτε συνήλθομεν ὡς βασιλεῖ **πολεμήσοντες** 2. 3. 21.

Nor did we come together with the intention of warring with the king.

272. Of Condition.
The circumstantial participle may express a condition. The negative is μή (cf. 340).

Νικῶντες μὲν τίνα ἂν ἀποκτείναιμεν; 2. 4. 6.

If we should conquer, whom should we kill?

Μὴ πορίσας ἄριστον 2. 3. 5.
Unless he provide breakfast.

273. Of Concession. — The circumstantial participle may express a concession. It is often accompanied by καί or καίπερ.

Οἱ δὲ βάρβαροι διαβεβηκότες τὸν Τίγρητα οὐ μέντοι καταφανεῖς ἦσαν 2. 4. 14.
And the barbarians, though they had crossed the Tigres, were nevertheless not in sight.

Θέλουσι καὶ πολλαπλάσιοι ὄντες μὴ δέχεσθαι ἡμᾶς 3. 2. 16.
They are not willing, though many times our number, to await our attack.

Προσεκύνησαν καίπερ εἰδότες ὅτι ἐπὶ θάνατον ἄγοιτο 1. 6. 10.
They did him reverence, although they knew that he was being led to death.

274. Of Attendant Circumstance. — The circumstantial participle may express a mere attendant circumstance.

Πρόξενος δὲ παρῆν ἔχων ὁπλίτας 1. 2. 3.
And Proxenus was there with hoplites.

Ξύλα σχίζων τις, ὡς εἶδε Κλέαρχον διελαύνοντα, ἵησι τῇ ἀξίνῃ 1. 5. 12.
And one who was splitting wood, when he saw Clearchus riding through, hurled his ax at him.

275. Of the Same Action. — The circumstantial participle and the leading verb may describe different aspects of the same action (cf. 194).

Καίτοι ταῦτα πράττων τί ἐποίει; Dem. 9. 15.
And yet, in doing this, what was he doing?

Δίκην ἐδίδοσαν κακῶς σκηνοῦντες 4. 4. 14.
They paid the penalty in being badly quartered.

276. The Circumstantial Participle in Absolute Constructions. — The circumstantial participle, when not in agreement with any word in the main part of the sentence, may be used in the genitive or accusative absolute to express many of the same relations as those above, *i.e. time, cause,* etc.

277. The Genitive Absolute. — A noun (or pronoun) and a participle are put in the genitive absolute, if the noun stands in no case-relation to any word in the main part of the sentence.

Κελεύοντος Κύρου ἔλαβον τῆς ζώνης τὸν Ὀρόνταν 1. 6. 10.
At the command of Cyrus they took Orontas by the girdle.

Ἅτε θεωμένων τῶν ἑταίρων πολλὴ φιλονικία ἐγίγνετο 4. 8. 27.
Since their comrades were watching, the rivalry grew intense.

Τοῦτο δὲ λέγοντος αὐτοῦ πτάρνυταί τις 3. 2. 9.
As he was saying this, some one sneezed.

278. The Accusative Absolute. — The participles of impersonal verbs, *e.g.* ἐξόν, δέον, παρόν, etc., and ὄν (with a neuter adjective), are put in the accusative absolute.

Τί δὴ ὑμᾶς ἐξὸν ἀπολέσαι οὐκ ἐπὶ τοῦτο ἤλθομεν; 2. 5. 22.
Why then, when it was possible to destroy you, did we not go at it?

Δόξαν δὲ ταῦτα ἐκήρυξαν οὕτω ποιεῖν 4. 1. 13.
This being voted, they proclaimed that they should do so.

Ὡς ὁπόταν σημήνῃ τοξεύειν δεῆσον 5. 2. 12.
On the ground that, when the signal was given, it would be necessary to shoot.

THE SUPPLEMENTARY PARTICIPLE

279. Two Uses of the Supplementary Participle. — The supplementary participle completes the notion of the leading verb. It has two uses: (a) not in indirect discourse it is closely parallel to the complementary infinitive (247); (b) as a form of indirect discourse it is parallel to the indirect discourse infinitive (242). In either use it may agree either with the subject or the object of the leading verb.

(a) Ἔχαιρε ταῦτα ἀκούων 7. 2. 4.
He rejoiced to hear this.
Εἶδε Κλέαρχον διελαύνοντα 1. 5. 12.
He saw Clearchus riding through.
(b) Ἴσθι μέντοι ἀνόητος ὤν 2. 1. 13.
But be assured you are a fool.
Ἤκουσε Κῦρον ἐν Κιλικίᾳ ὄντα 1. 4. 5.
He heard that Cyrus was in Cilicia.

Not in Indirect Discourse

280. With Verbs of Beginning, etc. — The supplementary participle follows verbs of *beginning, continuing, ceasing,* and the like, agreeing with the subject.

Πολεμῶν διεγένετο 2. 6. 5.   Οὔποτε ἐπαυόμην ἡμᾶς ... οἰκτίρων 3. 1. 19.
He continued fighting.   I never ceased pitying ourselves.
Ἀπείρηκα ἤδη συσκευαζόμενος καὶ βαδίζων 5. 1. 2.
I am tired now of packing up and walking.

281. With Verbs of Emotion. — The supplementary participle follows verbs of emotion, agreeing with the subject, or sometimes with the direct or indirect object.

Ἥδομαι μέν, ὦ Κλέαρχε, ἀκούων σου φρονίμους λόγους 2. 5. 16.
I am glad, Clearchus, to hear sensible words from you.
Πειθομένοις αὐτοῖς οὐ μεταμελήσει 7. 1. 34.
They will not repent of their obedience.

282. With Λανθάνω, etc. — The supplementary participle with λανθάνω, τυγχάνω, φθάνω, and a few other verbs, contains the leading idea of the expression.

Οὕτω τρεφόμενον ἐλάνθανεν αὐτῷ τὸ στράτευμα 1. 1. 9.
So the army was secretly supported for him.
Ὁ μὲν οὖν πρεσβύτερος παρὼν ἐτύγχανε 1. 1. 2.
Now the elder, as it chanced, was present.
Καὶ φθάνουσιν ἐπὶ τῷ ἄκρῳ γενόμενοι τοὺς πολεμίους 3. 4. 49.
And they arrived upon the height before the enemy.

Ἀμφότεροι ᾤχοντο κατὰ τῶν πετρῶν φερόμενοι 4. 7. 14.
Both went falling down the rocks.

283. With Φαίνομαι, etc. — The supplementary participle follows φαίνομαι and δῆλός εἰμι, in agreement with the subject.

Ἐπιορκῶν τε ἐφάνη καὶ τὰς σπονδὰς λύων 2. 5. 38.
He was manifestly both a perjurer and breaker of the truce.

Καὶ δῆλος ἦν ἀνιώμενος 1. 2. 11.
And he was evidently grieved.

284. With Verbs of Sense Perception. — The supplementary participle follows verbs of sense perception (cf. 287), and of *finding, detecting*, etc., in agreement with the object.

Ἰδὼν δὲ αὐτοὺς διαβαίνοντας 4. 3. 28.
And seeing them crossing.

Ἀκούουσι βοώντων τῶν στρατιωτῶν 4. 7. 24.
They hear the soldiers shouting.

Οὐχ εὑρήσετε ἐμὲ στασιάζοντα 6. 1. 29.
You will not find me revolting.

285. With Compounds of Ὁρῶ. — The supplementary participle follows περιορῶ (less commonly ἐφορῶ, εἰσορῶ), *overlook, allow*.

Νῦν οὕτω με ἄτιμον ὄντα ἐν τοῖς στρατιώταις τολμᾷς περιορᾶν; 7. 7. 46.
Do you now dare to allow me to be so dishonored in the presence of the soldiers?

286. Ἐμοὶ βουλομένῳ ἐστί. — The participles of βούλομαι and its synonyms follow εἰμί and γίγνομαι in agreement with the predicate dative (cf. 94).

Εἶπον οὐκ ἂν σφίσι βουλομένοις εἶναι Th. 7. 35.
They said that they would not be willing.

Ἡδομένοισιν ἡμῖν οἱ λόγοι γεγόνασι Hdt. 9. 46.
The proposals are acceptable to us.

In Indirect Discourse

287. With Verbs of Intellectual Perception. — The supplementary participle in indirect discourse follows verbs of intellectual perception (cf. 284), in agreement with either subject or object.

Ἤιδει γὰρ καὶ ἀπειρηκότας τοὺς στρατιώτας καὶ ἀσίτους ὄντας 2. 2. 16.
For he knew that the soldiers were wearied and without food.

Ἀκούων Κύρου ἔξω ὄντα τοῦ εὐωνύμου βασιλέα 1. 8. 13.
Hearing from Cyrus that the king was beyond the left wing.

Κατέμαθον ἀναστὰς μόλις καὶ τὰ σκέλη ἐκτείνας 5. 8. 14.
I observed that I rose and stretched my legs with difficulty.

THE VERBAL IN -Τέος

288. Two Constructions. — The verbal in -τέος, expressing necessity like the Latin participle in *-dus*, is used in a passive sense in two constructions, (a) personal and (b) impersonal.

(a) Πάντα ποιητέα 3. 1. 35.
Everything must be done.

(b) Πάντα ποιητέον 3. 1. 18.
Everything must be done.

289. The Personal Construction. — In the personal construction the verbal agrees with the subject, like any other predicate adjective (cf. 10).

Ποταμὸς ... ἡμῖν ἐστι διαβατέος 2. 4. 6.
A river must be crossed by us.

Τοσαῦτα δὲ ὄρη ὑμῖν ὁρᾶτε ὄντα πορευτέα 2. 5. 18.
And such great mountains you see which you must cross.

290. The Impersonal Construction. — In the impersonal construction the verbal is neuter singular or plural (-τέον or -τέα), and may take an object as if equivalent to δεῖ with the infinitive.

Τὴν μὲν πορείαν ... πέζῃ ποιητέον 6. 4. 12.
The march must be made on foot (= δεῖ ποιεῖσθαι τὴν πορείαν).

Ἱκανὸς δὲ καὶ ἐμποιῆσαι τοῖς παροῦσιν ὡς πειστέον εἴη Κλεάρχῳ 2. 6. 8.
Able also to impress upon those about him that Clearchus was to be obeyed.

Οὓς οὐ παραδοτέα τοῖς Ἀθηναίοις ἐστίν Th. 1. 86.
Who must not be handed over to the Athenians.

291. Agency with the Verbal. — The agent with the verbal is put in the dative (cf. 100), but with the impersonal construction it is sometimes accusative.

Πορευτέον δ' ἡμῖν τοὺς πρώτους σταθμοὺς ὡς ἂν δυνώμεθα μακροτάτους 2. 2. 12.
We must make the first marches as long as possible.

Ἰτέον ἂν εἴη θεασομένους (sc. ἡμᾶς) XM 3. 11. 1.
It would be best for us to go and see.

SEQUENCE OF MOODS AND TENSES

292. Tenses. — There is no law of sequence of tenses, as in Latin. Usually congruity of thought causes primary tenses to follow primary tenses, and secondary secondary, as in English. Still the point of view is free to shift.

Ἐπεὶ δὲ τετελεύτηκεν, ἀπαγγέλλετε Ἀριαίῳ ὅτι ἡμεῖς νικῶμέν τε βασιλέα καὶ ὡς ὁρᾶτε οὐδεὶς ἔτι ἡμῖν μάχεται 2. 1. 4.
But since he is dead, report to Ariaeus that we are victorious over the king, and, as you see, no one is fighting with us any longer.

Πλησίον ἦν ὁ σταθμὸς ἔνθα ἔμελλε καταλύειν 1. 8. 1.
The halting place was near, where he was to stop.

293. Sequence of Moods. — In certain dependent clauses there is a law of sequence of mood, distinguishing primary sequence from secondary sequence. Here primary tenses of the leading verb take primary sequence, and secondary tenses secondary sequence. But in final clauses and in indirect discourse primary sequence also is allowed with secondary tenses.

Λέγουσί τινες ὅτι πολλὰ ὑπισχνεῖ 1. 7. 5.
Some say that you make many promises.

Ἔλεγον ὅτι περὶ σπονδῶν ἥκοιεν 2. 3. 4.
They said that they had come about a truce.

Ἔλεγεν ὅτι τὸ στράτευμα ἀποδίδωσι 7. 6. 3 (here ἀποδιδοίη is possible).
He said that he gave back the army.

Ἔλεγον ὅτι Κῦρος μὲν τέθνηκεν 2. 1. 3 (here τεθνήκοι is possible).
They said that Cyrus was dead.

294. In Final Clauses. — In final clauses the subjunctive stands in primary sequence (217), the optative in secondary sequence (229).

Πάντα ποιητέα (*sc.* ἐστί) ὡς μήποτ' ἐπὶ τοῖς βαρβάροις γενώμεθα 3. 1. 35.
We must use all means never to fall into the barbarians' power.

Ἐκάλεσε γάρ τις αὐτὸν τῶν ὑπηρετῶν ὅπως ἴδοι τὰ ἱερά 2. 1. 9.
For one of the attendants called him to see the sacrifices.

Κατέκαυσεν ἵνα μὴ Κῦρος διαβῇ 1. 4. 18 (or διαβαίη).
He burned them that Cyrus might not cross.

295. In Conditions, Conditional Relative Clauses, etc. — In general (323, 324) and in future (315, 317) conditions, and in conditional relative and temporal clauses, the subjunctive, with ἐάν, ὃς ἄν, ὅταν, etc., stands in primary sequence, the optative, with εἰ, ὅς, ὅτε, etc., in secondary sequence (220, 221, 222, 232, 233, 234).

Κἂν μὲν ὑμᾶς ὁρῶσιν ἀθύμους, πάντες κακοὶ ἔσονται 3. 1. 36.
And if they see you disheartened, they will all be cowardly.

Πράττετε ὁποῖον ἄν τι ὑμῖν οἴησθε μάλιστα συμφέρειν 2. 2. 2.
Do whatever you think best.

Εἰ οὖν ὁρῴην ὑμᾶς σωτήριόν τι βουλευομένους, ἔλθοιμι ἄν 3. 3. 2.
Now if I should see you devising any salutary plan, I would come.

Εἷλκον δὲ τὰς νευρὰς ὁπότε τοξεύοιεν 4. 2. 28.
And they drew the strings when(ever) they shot.

296. In Indirect Discourse. — In the indirect discourse clause with ὅτι or ὡς, and in indirect questions, the moods of the direct form, in primary sequence, remain unchanged, in secondary sequence, become optatives (cf. 293).

Ἀπαγγέλλετε τοίνυν αὐτῷ ὅτι μάχης δεῖ 2. 3. 5.
Report to him then that a battle is necessary.

Εἰπὲ τίνα γνώμην ἔχεις 2. 2. 10.
Tell what opinion you have.

Ἔλεγεν ὅτι ἡ ὁδὸς ἔσοιτο πρὸς βασιλέα 1. 4. 11 (O. R. ἡ ὁδὸς ἔσται).
He said that the expedition was to be against the king.

Ὅ τι δὲ ποιήσοι οὐ διεσήμηνε 2. 1. 23.
But what he would do he did not declare (O. R. τί ποιήσεις;).

Τῷ δὲ Κύρῳ ἀπεκρίνατο ὅτι αὐτῷ μέλοι ὅπως καλῶς ἔχοι 1. 8. 13.
And he answered Cyrus that he was seeing to it that all should go well (O. R. ἐμοὶ μέλει ὅπως καλῶς ἔχῃ).

INDIRECT DISCOURSE

297. Finite Construction. — Indirect discourse is expressed as an object clause introduced by ὅτι or ὡς, after verbs of *saying*, *perceiving*, and *knowing*. Of the verbs of saying λέγω is usually so construed, εἶπον almost always, and φημί practically never.

Εἶπεν ὅτι βούλοιτο διαλεχθῆναι τοῖς ἄρχουσι 4. 4. 5.
He said that he wished to confer with the leaders.

Ἔγνω ὅτι οὐ δυνήσεται βιάσασθαι 1. 3. 2.
He perceived that he would not be able to compel them.

298. Infinitive Construction. — Indirect discourse is expressed as an object infinitive, with subject accusative, or without any subject expressed when it is the same as that of the leading verb (cf. 53), after some verbs of *saying*, *believing*, and *thinking*, always with ἡγοῦμαι, οἴομαι, νομίζω, δοκῶ, *think*, φημί, *say*.

Πρὸς τοῦτον οὖν ἔφη βούλεσθαι ἐλθεῖν 1. 3. 20.
He said that against him, therefore, he wished to go.

Νομίσας ἑτοίμους εἶναι αὐτῷ τοὺς ἱππέας 1. 6. 3.
Thinking that the horsemen were ready for him.

299. Participial Construction. — Indirect discourse is expressed as a participial clause after verbs of perception, such as *see, hear, perceive, know*, etc. The participle may be in agreement with either the subject or the object (287).

Ἐγίγνωσκον αὐτοὺς οἱ Ἕλληνες βουλομένους ἀπιέναι 3. 4. 36.
The Greeks knew that they wished to depart.

Σύνοιδα ἐμαυτῷ πάντα ἐψευσμένος αὐτόν 1. 3. 10.
I am conscious that I have deceived him in all things.

INDIRECT QUESTIONS

300. Moods and Tenses. — Questions indirectly quoted follow the same laws in regard to moods and tenses as the ὅτι-clause in indirect discourse (cf. 296).

Οὐκ ἴστε ὅ τι ποιεῖτε 1. 5. 16.
You do not know what you are doing.

Καὶ ὃς ἐθαύμασε τίς παραγγέλλει καὶ ἤρετο ὅ τι εἴη τὸ σύνθημα 1. 8. 16.
And he wondered who was giving out the watchword and asked what it was.

301. Simple Indirect Questions. — Simple indirect questions are introduced by εἰ, *whether*, by the interrogatives, indirect (ὅστις, ὅπου, ὁπότε, etc.) or direct (τίς, ποῦ, πότε, etc.), or by most relatives.

Ἤρετο εἴ τι παραγγέλλοι 1. 8. 15.
He asked whether he was giving any order.

Οἶδα γὰρ ὅπῃ οἴχονται 1. 4. 8.
For I know which way they have gone.

Ἤρετο τίς ὁ θόρυβος εἴη 1. 8. 16.   Δηλῶσαι δὲ ὧν δεόμεθα 3. 3. 14.
He asked what the noise was.   And to show us what we lack.

302. Compound Indirect Questions. — Compound indirect questions are introduced by πότερον (or πότερα) ... ἤ, εἴτε ... εἴτε, εἰ ... ἤ or εἴτε.

Θαυμάζω πότερα ὡς κρατῶν βασιλεὺς αἰτεῖ τὰ ὅπλα ἢ ὡς διὰ φιλίαν δῶρα
2. 1. 10.
I wonder whether the king asks for our arms as a conqueror or as gifts because of friendship.

Ἐβουλεύετο . . . εἰ πέμποιέν τινας ἢ πάντες ἴοιεν 1. 10. 5.
He took counsel whether they should send some or all should go.

RELATION OF INDIRECT TO DIRECT DISCOURSE

303. After Primary Tenses. — After ὅτι or ὡς, and in indirect questions, the moods and tenses in both principal and subordinate clauses remain unchanged when the leading verb is in a primary tense.

Ἐρεῖ οὐδεὶς ὡς ἐγώ, ἕως μὲν ἂν παρῇ τις, χρῶμαι 1. 4. 8.
No one shall say that I make use of a man, as long as any one stays by me (O. R. ἕως μὲν ἂν παρῇ τις, χρῆται).

304. After Secondary Tenses. — When the leading verb is in a secondary tense, primary tenses of the indicative or any subjunctive, in both principal and subordinate clauses, may be changed to the corresponding tenses of the optative, or may be retained unchanged (cf. 293).

Οἱ δ' ἔλεγον ὅτι τὰ μὲν πρὸς μεσημβρίαν τῆς ἐπὶ Βαβυλῶνα εἴη καὶ Μηδίαν, δι' ἧσπερ ἥκοιεν 3. 5. 15.
And they said that the region to the south lay on the road to Babylon and Media through which they had come (O. R. ἐστί, ἥκετε).

Ἔλεγον ὅτι Κῦρος μὲν τέθνηκεν, Ἀριαῖος δὲ πεφευγὼς . . . εἴη 2. 1. 3.
They said that Cyrus was dead and Ariaeus had fled (O. R. τέθνηκε, πέφευγε).

Εἶπεν ὅτι τὸ σύνθημα παρέρχεται δεύτερον ἤδη 1. 8. 16.
He said that the watchword was now passing along the second time.

305. Ὅτι with Direct Discourse. — Even the appropriate changes in the person of pronouns and of verbs may not be made, and then ὅτι or ὡς introduces what is practically direct discourse.

Ὁ δὲ ἀπεκρίνατο ὅτι οὐδ' εἰ γενοίμην, ὦ Κῦρε, σοί γ' ἂν ἔτι δόξαιμι 1. 6. 8.
And he replied: "Not even if I should become (your friend), O Cyrus, would I ever again seem so in *your* eyes."

Εἶπεν ὅτι αὐτός εἰμι ὃν ζητεῖς 2. 4. 16.
He said : " I am myself the man you seek."

306. Secondary Tenses after Secondary Tenses.

— When the leading verb is in a secondary tense, the secondary tenses of the indicative generally remain unchanged, but sometimes the imperfect and aorist (if it be the leading verb of the direct discourse) become respectively the present and the aorist optative.

Ἔγραψα ὅτι βασιλεὺς ἐξεπλάγη 2. 3. 1.
I wrote that the king was terrified (O. R. ἐξεπλάγη).

Ἔλεγεν ὅτι οὐκ ἄν ποτε προοῖτο, ἐπεὶ ἅπαξ φίλος αὐτοῖς ἐγένετο 1. 9. 10.
He said he would never abandon them when once he had become their friend (O. R. ἂν προοίμην, ἐγενόμην).

Ἐπήρετο αὐτὸν εἰ ὁπλιτεύοι 5. 8. 5.
Then he asked him whether he had been a hoplite (O. R. ὡπλίτευες ;).

307. Secondary Tenses in Unreal Conditions.

— The moods and tenses of unreal conditions (318, 321) remain unchanged in indirect discourse.

Ἴστε ὅτι οὐδ᾽ ἂν ἔγωγε ἐστασίαζον, εἰ ἄλλον εἵλεσθε 6. 1. 32.
Be sure that, if you had chosen another, I should not be in revolt either.

Λέγειν πρὸς Κλέανδρον ὡς οὐκ ἂν ἐποίησεν Ἀγασίας ταῦτα, εἰ μὴ ἐγὼ αὐτὸν ἐκέλευσα 6. 6. 15.
To say to Cleander that Agasias would not have done this unless I had bidden him.

308. Change of Present to Imperfect, etc.

— In Homer, after secondary tenses in indirect discourse the present and perfect indicative become imperfect and pluperfect respectively, as in English (cf. 292). The older usage survives occasionally, even in Attic.

Ἤισθετο ὅτι τὸ Μένωνος στράτευμα ἤδη ἐν Κιλικίᾳ ἦν 1. 2. 21.
He perceived that Menon's army was already in Cilicia (O. R. ἐστί).

Ἐπόρουσε . . . γιγνώσκων ὅ οἱ αὐτὸς ὑπείρεχε χεῖρας Ἀπόλλων Ε 433.
He rushed upon him, although he knew that Apollo himself was defending him (O. R. ὑπερέχει).

INFINITIVE AND PARTICIPIAL CONSTRUCTIONS

309. The Leading Verb. — In the infinitive and participial constructions of indirect discourse (cf. 298, 299) the leading verb of the direct discourse is put in the corresponding tense of the infinitive or participle (cf. 178 ff.).

Οἶμαι γὰρ ἂν οὐκ ἀχαρίστως μοι ἔχειν 2. 3. 18.
For I think it would not be a thankless task (O. R. οὐκ ἂν ἔχοι).

Ἐπεὶ ᾔσθετο διαβεβηκότας, ᾔσθη 1. 4. 16.
He was pleased when he perceived that they had crossed (O. R. διαβεβήκασι).

310. The Dependent Verbs. — The dependent verbs follow the same laws as after ὅτι or ὡς (303, 304).

Κατασχίσειν τε τὰς πύλας ἔφασαν, εἰ μὴ ἑκόντες ἀνοίξουσιν 7. 1. 16.
And they said they would burst in the gates if they (the others) did not voluntarily open them (O. R. κατασχίσομεν, ἀνοίξετε).

Ὁ δ' ὑπέσχετο ἀνδρὶ ἑκάστῳ δώσειν πέντε ἀργυρίου μνᾶς, ἐπὰν εἰς Βαβυλῶνα ἥκωσι 1. 4. 13.
And he promised to give each man five silver minae when they came to Babylon (O. R. δώσω, ἥκητε).

Εὔξαντο σωτήρια θύσειν, ἔνθα πρῶτον εἰς φιλίαν γῆν ἀφίκοιντο 5. 1. 1.
They vowed to sacrifice thank offerings for safety as soon as they came to a friendly country (O. R. θύσομεν, ἀφίκωμεν).

THE CONDITIONAL SENTENCE

311. Protasis and Apodosis. — Conditional sentences are made up of two parts, the principal clause, or apodosis, and the dependent clause, or protasis. The protasis usually, but not always, precedes.

Εἰ μὲν ὑμεῖς ἐθέλετε ἐξορμᾶν ἐπὶ ταῦτα, ἕπεσθαι ὑμῖν βούλομαι 3. 1. 25.
If you will take the initiative in this, I desire to follow you.

Καλῶς ἔσται, ἢν θεὸς θέλῃ 7. 3. 43.
It will be well, if God will.

312. Forms of the Protasis. — The protasis may be expressed by a conditional participle (272), or by a relative or temporal clause (221, 222, 233, 234) instead of a formal condition.

Ἄλλον μὲν ἑλόμενοι οὐχ εὑρήσετε ἐμὲ στασιάζοντα 6. 1. 29.
If you choose another, you will not find me in revolt.
Ὅ τι ἂν δέῃ πείσομαι 1. 3. 6.
Whatever may be necessary I will endure.

313. Particular and General Conditions. — Conditional sentences may be either particular (referring to a specific act or state), or general (including several or many specific acts or states in a general statement). In future conditions (315, 317), and in unreal conditions (318, 321), this distinction is not grammatically important; but for present and past general conditions distinct forms were developed.

Classification of Conditions

314. Present or Past Particular Conditions. — Present or past particular conditions take the appropriate tenses of the indicative in both clauses, with nothing implied as to fulfillment.

Εἰ οὖν βούλεσθε, ἔξεστιν ὑμῖν ἡμᾶς λαβεῖν συμμάχους 5. 4. 6.
Now if you wish, you can take us as allies.
Εἰ μὲν ἐπ' ἀγαθῷ ἐκόλασά τινα, ἀξιῶ ὑπέχειν δίκην 5. 8. 18.
If I chastised any one for his good, I deem it right to receive my deserts.
Cf. Οὓς (νεκρούς) δὲ μὴ εὕρισκον, κενοτάφιον αὐτοῖς ἐποίησαν μέγα 6. 4. 9.
And whatever (bodies) they did not find, for them they made a large cenotaph (cf. 312).

Future Conditions

315. The More Vivid Future Condition. — The more vivid future condition ('shall' condition) has ἐάν (ἄν, or ἤν) with the subjunctive (220) in the protasis, and some future form in the apodosis.

> Τί ἔσται τοῖς στρατιώταις, ἐὰν αὐτῷ ταῦτα χαρίσωνται; 2. 1. 10.
> What will the soldiers have, if they oblige him in this?
>
> Ἄλλους πέμψον, ἂν μή τινες ἐθελούσιοι φαίνωνται 4. 6. 19.
> Send others, if no volunteers appear.
>
> Cf. Ἐπειδὰν διαπράξωμαι ἃ δέομαι, ἥξω 2. 3. 29 (cf. 312).
> When I shall have accomplished what I desire, I will return.

316. Minatory or Monitory Form. — The protasis may also have εἰ with the future indicative. This generally has the effect of a threat or warning (minatory or monitory).

> Εἰ δέ πῃ τοῦτο ἔσται, τῇ ὅλῃ φάλαγγι κακὸν ἔσται 4. 8. 11.
> And if in any way this shall occur, it will be bad for the whole line.
>
> Εἰ δέ τινα ὑμῶν λήψομαι ἐν τῇ θαλάττῃ, καταδύσω 7. 2. 13.
> And if I shall catch any one of you on the sea, I will sink him.

317. The Less Vivid Future Condition. — The less vivid future condition (ideal, 'should' condition) has εἰ with the optative in the protasis (cf. 232), and the optative with ἄν in the apodosis (cf. 225).

> Πορευοίμεθα δ' ἂν οἴκαδε, εἴ τις ἡμᾶς μὴ λυποίη 2. 3. 23.
> We would march home, if no one should molest us.
>
> Εἴ σοι πάλιν βουλοίμην βοηθῆσαι, ἱκανὸς ἂν γενοίμην 7. 7. 38.
> If I should again desire to come to your aid, I would be able.
>
> Cf. Ὀκνοίην μὲν ἂν εἰς τὰ πλοῖα ἐμβαίνειν ἃ ἡμῖν δοίη 1. 3. 17 (cf. 312).
> I should hesitate to embark on the vessels which he would give us.

Unreal Conditions

318. Present Unreal Condition. — The present unreal condition (hypothetical, contrary to fact) states an hypothesis opposed to a present fact. It has εἰ with the imperfect indicative in the protasis, and the imperfect indicative with ἄν in the apodosis.

Εἰ μὲν ἠπιστάμεθα σαφῶς . . . οὐδὲν ἂν ἔδει ὧν μέλλω λέγειν 5. 1. 10.

If we were certain (the present fact is οὐκ ἐπιστάμεθα), there would be no need of what I am about to say.

Εἰ μὲν ἑώρων ἀποροῦντας ὑμᾶς, τοῦτ' ἂν ἐσκόπουν 5. 6. 30.

If I saw that you were in straits, I should consider this, etc.

Εἰ γὰρ ἐκήδου, ἧκες (cf. 136) ἂν φέρων πλήρη τὸν μισθόν 7. 5. 5.

For if you cared, you would have come, with full pay.

319. Impersonals without Ἄν. — With impersonals of *necessity, obligation*, etc., ἄν is not required in the apodosis. Such are χρῆν, or ἐχρῆν, ἔδει, ἐξῆν, εἰκὸς ἦν, etc.

Ἐξῆν ὑμῖν ἐπικουρεῖν αὐτοῖς, εἰ ἐβούλεσθε 5. 8. 21.

You could aid them, if you wished.

Αἰσχρὸν γὰρ ἦν τὰ μὲν ἐμὰ διαπεπρᾶχθαι 7. 7. 40.

For it would be base to have exacted mine own.

320. Present Unreal Condition in Homer. — In a present unreal condition, Homer uses the optative in both protasis and apodosis, not distinguishing it in form from the less vivid future condition.

Εἰ μὲν νῦν ἐπὶ ἄλλῳ ἀεθλεύοιμεν Ἀχαιοί, | ἦ τ' ἂν ἐγὼ τὰ πρῶτα λαβὼν κλισίηνδε φεροίμην Ψ 274.

If we Achaeans were now contending in honor of any one else, verily I should take the first prize and bear it to my tent.

321. The Past Unreal Condition. — The past unreal condition (hypothetical, contrary to fact) states an hypothesis opposed to a past fact. It generally has εἰ with the aorist indicative in the protasis, and the aorist indicative with ἄν in the apodosis. This form is established already in Homer.

Οὐκ ἂν ἐποίησεν Ἀγασίας ταῦτα, εἰ μὴ ἐγὼ αὐτὸν ἐκέλευσα 6. 6. 15.

Agasias would not have done this, if I had not commanded him (the past fact was αὐτὸν ἐκέλευσα).

Καί νύ κ' ἔτι πλέονας Λυκίων κτάνε δῖος Ὀδυσσεύς, | εἰ μὴ ἄρ' ὀξὺ νόησε μέγας κορυθαίολος Ἕκτωρ Ε 679.

And now the godlike Odysseus would have slain still more of the Lycians, had not the mighty, gleaming-crested Hector quickly perceived him.

Cf. Ὁπότερον τούτων ἐποίησεν, οὐδενὸς ἂν ἧττον Ἀθηναίων πλούσιοι ἦσαν
   Lys. 32. 23 (cf. 312).
Whichever of these (things) he had done, they would be no less rich than any of the Athenians.

322. Use of Imperfect or Pluperfect. — The imperfect or pluperfect indicative may be used in either clause of a past unreal condition to express continuance or completion respectively.

Εἰ δὲ τοῦτο πάντες ἐποιοῦμεν, ἅπαντες ἂν ἀπωλόμεθα 5. 8. 13.
And if we had all acted in that way, we should all have perished.

Οὐ γὰρ ἂν ἥψατ' αὐτῶν παρόντων ἡμῶν (= εἰ ἡμεῖς παρῆμεν), ἢ οὐκ ἂν ὡρκίζομεν αὐτόν, ὥστε τῆς εἰρήνης διημαρτήκει, καὶ οὐκ ἂν ἀμφότερα εἶχε, καὶ τὴν εἰρήνην καὶ τὰ χωρία Dem. 18. 30.
For, had we been there, he would not have laid hands on them, or else we would have refused to administer the oaths to him, so that he would have missed the peace, and would not have secured both, viz., the peace and the strongholds.

General Conditions

323. Present General Condition. — The present general condition has ἐάν (ἄν or ἤν) with the subjunctive (cf. 220) in the protasis, and a present indicative or its equivalent in the apodosis.

Τὰς δὲ ὠτίδας, ἄν τις ταχὺ ἀνιστῇ, ἔστι λαμβάνειν 1. 5. 3.
Bustards, if one rouse them suddenly, may be caught.

Ἀδικοῦντα, ἢν λάβῃς, κολάζεις; XC. 3. 1. 11.
Do you punish a wrong-doer, if you catch him?

Cf. Οἱ δὲ ἄνδρες εἰσὶν οἱ ποιοῦντες ὅ τι ἂν ἐν ταῖς μάχαις γίγνηται 3. 2. 18.
But men are the doers of whatever is done in battles.

324. Past General Condition. — The past general condition has εἰ with the optative (cf. 232) in the protasis and the imperfect or its equivalent in the apodosis.

Εἰ δὲ δή ποτε πορεύοιτο καὶ πλεῖστοι μέλλοιεν ὄψεσθαι, προσκαλῶν τοὺς φίλους ἐσπουδαιολογεῖτο 1. 9. 28.

And if ever he was on the march, and very many were likely to see it, he called his friends to him and engaged them in conversation.

Cf. Ὁπόσα λαμβάνοι πλοῖα, **κατῆγεν** 5. 1. 16 (cf. 312).

Whatever vessels he captured, he brought to land.

325. Mixed Forms. — It is not uncommon to find conditions in which the protasis is of one type and the apodosis of another.

Ἢν οὖν ἔλθωμεν ἐπ' αὐτοὺς (315) πρὶν φυλάξασθαι, ... μάλιστα ἂν λάβοιμεν (317) καὶ ἀνθρώπους καὶ χρήματα 7. 3. 35.

If, therefore, we come upon them before they place their guards, we should be most likely to capture both men and goods.

Οὐδ' ἂν ἔγωγε ἐστασίαζον (321), εἰ ἄλλον εἵλεσθε (324) 6. 1. 32.

Nor would I for my part be in revolt, if you had chosen another.

THE PARTICLE Ἄν

326. Two Uses of Ἄν. — The particle ἄν has two distinct uses: (*a*) in apodosis, where it belongs to the leading verb, and (*b*) in protasis, where it belongs to the introductory word of the dependent clause.

The Ἄν of Apodosis

327. With the Optative and Secondary Tenses of the Indicative. — Ἄν is used with the secondary tenses of the indicative and with the optative to denote contingency.

Οὐδ' ἂν συνηκολούθησά σοι 7. 7. 11.

Nor would I have followed you.

Ἐγὼ γὰρ ὀκνοίην μὲν ἂν εἰς τὰ πλοῖα ἐμβαίνειν 1. 3. 17.

For I should hesitate to embark on the boats.

328. Iterative Ἄν. — Ἄν is also used with the imperfect and aorist indicative to denote customary or intermittent action.

Διηρώτων ἄν αὐτοὺς τί λέγοιεν Pl. Ap. 22 b.
I was wont to ask them what they meant.

Οὐδένα ἄν πώποτε ἀφείλετο, ἀλλ' ἀεὶ πλείω προσεδίδου 1. 9. 19.
He was never wont to take from any one, but always to add more

329. With Future Indicative, etc., in Homer. — Homer uses ἄν (κέ) with the future indicative, the subjunctive, or the optative, in a principal clause nearly or quite like a simple future (216, 227).

Ὁ δέ κεν κεχολώσεται ὅν κεν ἵκωμαι A 139.
And he will be angry to whom I shall come.

Εἰ δέ κε μὴ δώῃσιν, ἐγὼ δέ κεν αὐτὸς ἕλωμαι A 324.
And if he do not give her up, I will myself take her.

Νῦν γάρ κεν ἕλοι πόλιν B 12.
For now he will (can) take the city.

330. The Ἄν of Apodosis Retained. — The ἄν of apodosis is retained in indirect discourse, and in general when finite forms with ἄν are changed to infinitives or participles.

Ἀναρχίᾳ ἄν καὶ ἀταξίᾳ ἐνόμιζον ἡμᾶς ἀπολέσθαι 3. 2. 29.
They thought that we should be ruined by lack of order and of discipline (O. R. ἄν ἀπόλοιντο).

Ἀλλὰ σιωπῶ, πόλλ' ἄν ἔχων εἰπεῖν Dem. 3. 27.
Of other things I am silent, though I might have much to say.

The Ἄν of Protasis

331. In Conditions, Conditional Relative Clauses, etc. — Ἄν is used in dependent clauses, joined to the connectives εἰ, ὅς, ὅτε, etc., and followed by the subjunctive (220, 221, 222).

Ἢν οὖν σωφρονῆτε, τούτῳ δώσετε ὅ τι ἄν ἔχητε 7. 3. 17.
If therefore you are wise, you will give him whatever you have.

Ὅπου ἄν ὦ 1. 3. 6.   Περιμένετε ἔστ' ἄν ἐγὼ ἔλθω 5. 1. 4.
Wherever I may be.   Wait till I come.

332. In Final Clauses. — Occasionally ἄν is also joined to the final particles ὡς, ὅπως (ὄφρα), in primary sequence.

Χρὴ ... προσέχειν τὸν νοῦν, ὡς ἂν τὸ παραγγελλόμενον δύνησθε ποιεῖν 6. 3. 18.
It is necessary to take heed, that you may be able to do what is ordered.

Διὰ τῆς σῆς χώρας ἄξεις ἡμᾶς ὅπως ἂν εἰδῶμεν XC 5. 2. 21.
You will lead us through your country in order that we may know.

333. The Ἄν of Protasis Lost. — When the subjunctive of these clauses (331, 332) becomes optative in indirect discourse (304), ἄν is lost.

Εὔξαντο σωτήρια θύσειν, ἔνθα πρῶτον εἰς φιλίαν γῆν ἀφίκοιντο 5. 1. 1.
They vowed to sacrifice thank offerings for safety as soon as they came to a friendly land (O. R. ἔνθα ἂν ἀφικώμεθα).

THE NEGATIVES

334. Οὐ and Μή. — There are two negative adverbs, οὐ and μή, with corresponding compounds, οὔτε, οὐδέ, οὐδείς, οὔποτε, etc.; μήτε, μηδέ, μηδείς, μήποτε, etc. In general οὐ is the negative of *fact*, μή the negative of *will*. The laws governing the use of the simple forms apply also to their compounds.

In Independent Sentences

335. Indicative and Optative. — The indicative and optative take οὐ, except in wishes and in negative questions that expect the answer *no*.

Πλοῖα δὲ ἡμεῖς οὐκ ἔχομεν 2. 2. 3.
But boats we have not.

Οὐκ ἂν οὖν θαυμάζοιμι 3. 2. 35.
Therefore I should not be surprised.

Οὐκ ἐπιστάμεθα; 2. 4. 3.
Do we not understand?

Μὴ γένοιτο Dem. 28. 21.
God forbid!

Ἆρα μὴ διαβάλλεσθαι δόξεις; XM. 2. 6. 34.
You will not think yourself slandered, will you?

336. Subjunctive and Imperative with Μή. — The subjunctive and imperative always take μή.

Μὴ μέλλωμεν 3. 1. 46.   Μὴ θαυμάζετε 1. 3. 3.
Let us not delay.   Marvel not.

Μηδὲ μέντοι τοῦτο μεῖον δόξητε ἔχειν 3. 2. 17.
But do not suppose, however, that you are the worse off for this.

In Dependent Clauses

337. Clauses with Οὐ. — Causal clauses, indicative result clauses (cf. 202), and ὅτι or ὡς indirect discourse clauses take οὐ. Relative and temporal clauses take οὐ, save when conditional or general (221, 222, 233, 234).

Ἠτιᾶτο αὐτὸν ὅτι οὐχ ὑπέμεινεν 4. 1. 19.
He blamed him because he had not waited.

Ὥστε βασιλεὺς τὴν μὲν πρὸς ἑαυτὸν ἐπιβουλὴν οὐκ ᾐσθάνετο 1. 1. 8.
So that the king did not perceive the plot against him.

Διδάσκειν σε βούλομαι ὡς σὺ ἡμῖν οὐκ ὀρθῶς ἀπιστεῖς 2. 5. 6.
I wish to show you that you are not right in distrusting us.

Ὃ οὐ δυνατόν ἐστιν 1. 3. 17.
Which is not possible.

Ἐπεὶ δὲ οὐδεὶς ἀντέλεγεν, εἶπεν . . . 3. 2. 38.
And when no one spoke in opposition, he said . . .

Cf. Οἳ μὴ ἔτυχον ἐν ταῖς τάξεσιν ὄντες 2. 2. 14.
Whoever were not, as it chanced, in the ranks.

338. Clauses with Μή. — Conditional clauses, final clauses (including the final relative clause, 205) take μή, but after verbs of *fear*, μή, *lest*, is followed by οὐ.

Εἰ μὴ ὑμεῖς ἤλθετε 2. 1. 4.
If you had not come.

Ἂν δέ τις μὴ ποιῇ ταῦτα, τῇ θεῷ μελήσει 5. 3. 13.
And if any one fail to do this, it will be the concern of the goddess.

Ἠνάγκασα δὲ σὲ τοῦτον ἄγειν ὡς **μὴ** ἀπόλοιτο 5. 8. 8.
And I forced you to carry him that he might not perish.

Δείσας μὴ **οὐ** πρῶτος παραδράμοι εἰς τὸ χωρίον 4. 7. 11.
Fearing that he might not get by first into the place.

With the Infinitive and Participle

339. The Infinitive. — The infinitive regularly takes μή, save in indirect discourse, where οὐ is the general rule.

Εἰ μέλλομεν τούτους εἴργειν ὥστε **μὴ** δύνασθαι βλάπτειν ἡμᾶς 3. 3. 16.
If we are to hinder them from being able to injure us.

Οἶμαι γὰρ ἂν **οὐκ** ἀχαρίστως μοι ἔχειν 2. 3. 18.
For I think it would not be a thankless task.

Ἐβόων δὲ ἀλλήλοις **μὴ** θεῖν δρόμῳ 1. 8. 19 (O. R. μὴ θέωμεν, 336).
They shouted to one another not to go on a run.

340. The Participle. — The participle regularly takes οὐ, save when conditional (272), or equivalent to a general relative clause.

Οὐ πολὺ δὲ προεληλυθότων αὐτῶν ἐπιφαίνεται πάλιν 3. 3. 6.
And when they had advanced a little way, he again appeared.

Μὴ πορίσας ἄριστον 2. 3. 5.
Unless he provide breakfast.

Οἱ **μὴ** δυνάμενοι διατελέσαι τὴν ὁδὸν ἐνυκτέρευσαν ἄσιτοι 4. 5. 11.
Those who could not finish the journey passed the night without food.

Redundant Negatives

341. After Verbs of Hindering, etc. — After verbs and phrases containing a negative idea, such as *hindering, forbidding, denying*, a redundant μή is often placed before the infinitive.

Ἀποκωλῦσαι τοὺς Ἕλληνας **μὴ** ἐλθεῖν εἰς τὴν Φρυγίαν 6. 4. 24.
To prevent the Greeks from entering Phrygia.

Μικρὸν ἐξέφυγε **μὴ** καταπετρωθῆναι 1. 3. 2.
He narrowly escaped being stoned to death.

342. Μὴ οὐ. — After these verbs and phrases, when themselves accompanied by a negative adverb, the double negative μὴ οὐ commonly precedes the infinitive.

Οὐ δυνατοὶ αὐτὴν ἴσχειν εἰσὶ Ἀργεῖοι μὴ οὐκ ἐξιέναι Hdt. 9. 12.
The Argives cannot restrain her from going out.

Τί ἐμποδὼν μὴ οὐχὶ . . . ἀποθανεῖν; 3. 1. 13.
What prevents (*i.e.* nothing prevents) their being killed?

343. Οὐ μή. — The aorist subjunctive (cf. 215) or the future indicative is used with οὐ μή as an emphatic negative future.

Τὰ μὲν γὰρ ξένια οὐ μὴ γένηται τῇ στρατιᾷ τριῶν ἡμερῶν σῖτα 6. 2. 4.
For the hospitable gifts will not provision the army for three days.

Τοὺς . . . πονηροὺς οὐ μή ποτε βελτίους ποιήσετε Aes. 3. 177.
You will never make the wicked better.

344. Repetition of Negative. — A negative followed by one or more compound negatives is strengthened, but followed by the simple form is destroyed as in English.

Μετὰ ταῦτα οὔτε ζῶντα Ὀρόνταν οὔτε τεθνηκότα οὐδεὶς εἶδε πώποτε οὐδὲ ὅπως ἀπέθανεν οὐδεὶς εἰδὼς ἔλεγεν 1. 6. 11.
After this no one ever saw Orontas, either alive or dead, nor could any one tell with certainty how he died.

Οὐδεὶς οὐκ ἔπασχέ τι XS 1. 9.
Every one (no one not) was affected.

THE PREPOSITIONS

WITH ONE CASE

345. Prepositions governing the Genitive. — With the genitive only: ἀντί, *instead of;* ἀπό, *from, away from;* ἐκ or ἐξ, *from, out of;* πρό, *before.*

Κῦρον εἵλοντο ἀντὶ Τισσαφέρνους 1. 9. 9.
They chose Cyrus instead of Tissaphernes.

Καταπηδήσας ἀπὸ τοῦ ἅρματος 1. 8. 3.
Leaping down from the chariot.

Ἐκ Φοινίκης ἐλαύνων 1. 7. 12. Πρὸ τῆς μάχης 1. 7. 13.
Marching out of Phoenicia. Before the battle.

346. Adverbial Prepositions with the Genitive. — With the genitive are construed also the adverbial prepositions ἄνευ, ἄτερ, *without;* ἄχρι, μέχρι, *up to, until;* μεταξύ, *between;* ἕνεκα, *on account of;* πλήν, *except.*

Ἄνευ τῆς Κύρου γνώμης 1. 3. 13. Μέχρι τοῦ Μηδίας τείχους 1. 7. 15.
Without the approval of Cyrus. Up to the wall of Media.

Μεταξὺ τοῦ ποταμοῦ καὶ τῆς τάφρου 1. 7. 15.
Between the river and the ditch.

Χρημάτων ἕνεκα 1. 9. 17. Πάντες πλὴν Κύρου 1. 8. 6.
On account of money. All except Cyrus.

347. Prepositions governing the Dative. — With the dative only: ἐν, *in;* σύν or ξύν, *with.* The latter is much used by Xenophon, sparingly by other authors.

Ἐν δὲ τῷ τρίτῳ σταθμῷ 1. 7. 1. Σὺν στρατεύματι πολλῷ 1. 8. 1.
And in the third day's march. With a large army.

348. Prepositions governing the Accusative. — With the accusative only: εἰς or ἐς, *into, to.*

Εἰς τὸ ἐρυμνὸν χωρίον ἡγοῦντο 6. 5. 1. Ἐξελαύνει εἰς Πέλτας 1. 2. 10.
They led the way into the stronghold. He marches to Peltae.

Εἰς μάχην παρεσκευασμένος 1. 8. 1. Λέγειν εἰς ὑμᾶς 5. 6. 28.
Prepared for battle. To speak to you.

349. Adverbial Preposition with the Accusative. — With the accusative is construed also the adverbial preposition ὡς, *to.* It is used with persons only.

Πορεύεται ὡς βασιλέα 1. 2. 4. (Οἴχεται) ὡς Σεύθην 7. 7. 55.
He proceeds to the king. (He has gone off) to Seuthes.

PREPOSITIONS WITH TWO CASES

350. Genitive and Accusative. — With the genitive and accusative: διά, (g.) *through,* (a.) *on account of;* κατά, (g.) *down from,* (a.) *down along, by;* ὑπέρ, (g.) *above, in behalf of,* (a.) *over, beyond.*

Διὰ ταύτης τῆς χώρας 1. 5. 4.
Through this country.

Δι' εὔνοιάν τε καὶ πιστότητα 1. 8. 29.
On account of good will and fidelity.

Κατὰ τῶν πετρῶν φερόμενοι 4. 7. 14.
Falling down from the rocks.

Κατὰ γῆν καὶ κατὰ θάλατταν 1. 1. 7.
By land and by sea.

Μαστὸς ἦν ὑπὲρ αὐτῶν 4. 2. 6.
There was a hill above them.

Μαχόμενοι ὑπὲρ Κύρου 1. 9 31.
Fighting in behalf of Cyrus.

Δι' ὅλης τῆς νυκτός 4. 2. 4.
Throughout the whole night.

Δι' ἄνδρα δειλόν 6. 6. 24.
On account of a coward.

Κατὰ πρανοῦς γηλόφου 1. 5. 8.
Down a steep hill.

Κατὰ τὰ παρηγγελμένα 2. 2. 8.
According to orders.

Ἡ κατ' ἐνιαυτὸν πρόσοδος 7. 7. 36.
The yearly revenue.

Τοὺς ὑπὲρ τετταράκοντα ἔτη 5. 3. 1.
Those over forty years of age.

351. Dative and Accusative. — With the dative and accusative: ἀνά, (d. poetic) *upon;* (a.) *up along, upon.*

Χρυσέῳ ἀνὰ σκήπτρῳ A 15.
Upon a golden staff.

Ἐλαύνων ἀνὰ κράτος 1. 8. 1.
Riding at full speed.

Οἰκεῖν ἀνὰ τὰ ὄρη 3. 5. 16.
To dwell upon the mountains.

Ἔστησαν ἀνὰ ἑκατόν 5. 4. 12.
They stood by hundreds.

PREPOSITIONS WITH THREE CASES

352. Ἀμφί. — Ἀμφί, (g.) *about* (rare in prose), (d.) *about* (poetic), (a.) *about.*

Ἀμφὶ ὧν εἶχον διαφερόμενοι 4. 5. 17.
Quarreling about what they had.

Ἀμφὶ τὰ εἴκοσι 1. 7. 10.
About twenty.

Τελαμὼν ἀμφὶ στήθεσσιν B 388.
The strap about the breast.

Οἱ ἀμφ' αὐτούς 1. 8. 27.
Their followers (cf. 356).

353. Ἐπί. — Ἐπί, (g.) *upon,* (d.) *on, at, in the power of,* (a.) *up to, against.*

Ἐπὶ ἁμαξῶν 1. 7. 20.
On wagons.

Ἔκειντο ἐπ' αὐτῷ 1. 8. 27.
They lay upon him.

Ἴετο ἐπ' αὐτόν 1. 8. 26.
He rushed upon him.

Ἐπὶ τοῦ εὐωνύμου 1. 8. 9.
On the left wing.

Ἐπὶ ταῖς βασιλέως θύραις 1. 9. 3.
At the king's court.

Ἀναβὰς ἐπὶ τὸν ἵππον 1. 8. 3.
Mounting on his horse.

354. Μετά. — Μετά, (g.) *with*, (d. poetic) *among*, (a.) *after*.

Οἱ μετὰ Κύρου 1. 8. 7. Μετὰ δὲ τριτάτοισιν ἄνασσεν A 252.
Those with Cyrus. And he ruled among the third generation.

Μετὰ τὴν μάχην 1. 7. 13. Μετὰ τοῦτον ἄλλος ἀνέστη 1. 3. 15.
After the battle. After him another arose.

355. Παρά. — Παρά, (g.) *from, beside, from,* (d.) *beside, near,* (a.) *to the presence of, to, beside, contrary to.*

Παρὰ μὲν Κύρου δούλου ὄντος οὐδεὶς ἀπῄει 1. 9. 29.
No one would depart from Cyrus although he was a subject.

Παρ' ἐκείνῳ γὰρ ἦν 1. 8. 27. Ἦν παρὰ τὴν ὁδὸν κρήνη 1. 2. 13.
For he was near him. There was a spring by the roadside.

Εἰσῇσαν δὲ παρ' αὐτὸν 1. 7. 8. Παρὰ τὰς σπονδάς 1. 9. 8.
And they came in to him. Contrary to the truce.

356. Περί. — Περί, (g.) *about, concerning,* (d.) *about, around,* (a.) *about, near.*

Περὶ τούτων λέγειν 1. 9. 23. Περὶ μέσας νύκτας 1. 7. 1.
To speak concerning these things. About midnight.

Στρεπτοὺς περὶ τοῖς τραχήλοις 1. 5. 8. Τῶν περὶ αὐτόν 1. 8. 27.
Necklaces about their necks. Of his followers (cf. 352).

357. Πρός. — Πρός, (g.) *in front of, from,* (d.) *at, by, in addition to,* (a.) *to, toward, against.*

Ἔπαινον πολὺν πρὸς ὑμῶν 7. 6. 33. Πρὸς αὐτῷ τῷ στρατεύματι 1. 8. 14.
Much praise from you. By (near) the army itself.

Ἀφειστήκεσαν πρὸς Κῦρον 1. 1. 6. Πρὸς δ' ἄρκτον 1. 7. 6.
They had revolted to Cyrus. And toward the north.

358. Ὑπό. — Ὑπό, (g.) *by* (of agent), *under,* (d.) *under, at the foot of,* (a.) (*to a place*) *under, towards.*

Ἐτετίμητο γὰρ ὑπὸ Κύρου 1. 8. 29. Ὑπὸ τῇ ἀκροπόλει 1. 2. 8.
For he had been honored by Cyrus. At the foot of the acropolis.

Αὐτὸν ἀκοντίζει τις παλτῷ ὑπὸ τὸν ὀφθαλμόν 1. 8. 27.
Some one strikes him with a javelin under the eye.

THE CONJUNCTIONS

359. Coördination and Subordination. — Greek is a syndetic language, abounding in connectives. Asyndeton, common in English, is comparatively uncommon in Greek. Connectives are of two kinds, **coördinating conjunctions**, which join sentences, clauses, or words, of equal grammatical value (**Parataxis**), and **subordinating conjunctions**, which join sentences or clauses of unequal grammatical value (**Hypotaxis**).

COÖRDINATING CONJUNCTIONS

360. Classification. — The most common coördinating conjunctions are the enclitic and post-positive τέ (and its compounds εἴτε, οὔτε, and μήτε), καί (καίτοι), ἤ (ἤτοι), and the post-positives γάρ, δέ (οὐδέ, μηδέ, not post-positive), δή, μέν (μέντοι), οὖν, and τοίνυν. Coördinating conjunctions may be grouped as **copulative, disjunctive, adversative**, and **inferential**.

COPULATIVE CONJUNCTIONS

361. Singly. — The copulative conjunctions used singly are καί, *and;* τέ, *and*, not common in prose; δέ, *and*, with more or less adversative force; after a negative οὐδέ, μηδέ, *and not, nor*.

Κατέκαον τὰς ἀμάξας καὶ τὰς σκηνάς 3. 3. 1.
They burned the wagons and the tents.

Τόξ᾽ ὤμοισιν ἔχων ἀμφηρεφέα τε φαρέτρην A 45.
With a bow on his shoulders and a covered quiver.

Ἀναστὰς δὲ πάλιν εἶπε 3. 2. 34.
And rising again he said.

Οὐδ᾽ εἰς τὸ τεῖχος τοὺς ἀσθενοῦντας ἐδέχοντο 5. 5. 6.
Nor would they receive the sick into the fortress.

362. As Correlatives. — The copulative conjunctions used as correlatives are τέ — καί, καί — καί, τέ — τέ, *both — and*, the last particularly common in Homer; οὔτε — οὔτε, μήτε — μήτε, *neither — nor;* or the second clause may be positive (οὔτε — τέ).

Ἄρχειν τε καὶ ἄρχεσθαι 1. 9. 4.
Both to rule and to be ruled.

Τά τε ἱερὰ ἡμῖν καλὰ οἵ τε οἰωνοὶ αἴσιοι τά τε σφάγια κάλλιστα 6. 5. 21.
The sacrifices are favorable to us, the omens propitious, and the victims most favorable.

Καὶ κατὰ γῆν καὶ κατὰ θάλατταν 3. 2. 13.
Both by land and by sea.

Οὔτε γὰρ ἀγορὰ ἔστιν ἱκανὴ οὔτε ὅτου ὠνησόμεθα εὐπορία 5. 1. 6.
For there is neither an adequate market, nor means wherewith to buy.

Ὤμοσαν . . . μήτε προδώσειν ἀλλήλους σύμμαχοί τε ἔσεσθαι 2. 2. 8.
They swore both not to betray one another and to be allies.

DISJUNCTIVE CONJUNCTIONS

363. Singly. — The only disjunctive conjunction used singly is ἤ, *or*, which is also used as a comparative conjunction, *than*.

Σπονδὰς ἢ πόλεμον ἀπαγγελῶ; 2. 1. 23.
Am I to report a truce or war?

Μισθὸς πλέον ἢ τριῶν μηνῶν 1. 2. 11.
Pay for more than three months.

364. As Correlatives. — The disjunctive conjunctives used as copulatives are ἤ (ἤτοι) — ἤ, *either — or;* εἴτε — εἴτε, *whether — or;* negative οὔτε — οὔτε, μήτε — μήτε, *neither — nor;* οὐδέ — οὐδέ, μηδέ — μηδέ, *not even — nor yet.*

Ἢ ἀποσκάπτει τι ἢ ἀποτειχίζει 2. 4. 4.
He is either digging some ditch or building some wall.

Βουλεύεσθαι εἴτε τήμερον εἴτε αὔριον δοκεῖ ὑπερβάλλειν τὸ ὄρος 4. 6. 8.
To plan whether it seems best to-day or to-morrow to cross the mountain.

Οὔτε ἀποδεδράκασιν . . . οὔτε ἀποπεφεύγασιν 1. 4. 8.
They have neither run away (by stealth) nor escaped (by rapid flight).

Σύγε οὐδὲ ὁρῶν γιγνώσκεις, οὐδὲ ἀκούων μέμνησαι 3. 1. 27.
As for you, not even when you see do you understand, nor yet when you hear do you remember.

ADVERSATIVE CONJUNCTIONS

365. Singly.—The adversative conjunctions, used singly, are ἀλλά, δέ, *but;* μέντοι, *however;* καίτοι, *and yet.*

Οὐκ ἔφυγεν, ἀλλὰ διήλασε παρὰ τὸν ποταμόν 1. 10. 7.
He did not flee, but marched along the river.

Εἰ δέ τις ἄλλο ὁρᾷ βέλτιον, λεξάτω 3. 2. 38.
But if any one sees another (and a) better plan, let him speak.

Οἱ μέντοι πολέμιοι οὐδὲν ἐπαύσαντο 4. 2. 4.
The enemy, however, did not cease at all.

Καίτοι ἔχω γε αὐτῶν καὶ τέκνα καὶ γυναῖκας 1. 4. 8.
And yet I hold both their wives and children.

366. As Correlatives.—The adversative conjunctions used as correlatives are μέν — δέ (μέντοι), *on the one hand — on the other hand,* but any translation of μέν is either too emphatic or too formal.

Οἱ μὲν ᾤχοντο, Κλέαρχος δὲ περιέμενε 2. 1. 6.
They went off, but Clearchus remained.

Αὐτὸν ἔπαισε μέν, ἔδησε δ' οὔ 4. 6. 2.
He beat him, indeed, but did not bind him.

Δοκεῖ μὲν κἀμοὶ ταῦτα · οὐ μέντοι ταχύ γε ἀπαγγελῶ 2. 3. 9.
This seems best to me also, but still I shall not announce it, at least immediately.

INFERENTIAL CONJUNCTIONS

367. The most important inferential conjunctions are γάρ, *for,* frequent in the combinations καὶ γάρ, ἀλλὰ γάρ; οὖν, οὐκοῦν, τοίνυν, *therefore, then;* δή, *now, then,* frequent in the combination καὶ δὴ καί.

Οἱ γὰρ στρατιῶται οὗτοι πάντες πρὸς ὑμᾶς βλέπουσι 3. 1. 36.
For all these soldiers look to you.

Καὶ γὰρ ὁμίχλη ἐγένετο 4. 2. 7.
(And with reason) for a mist arose.

Ἴσως οὖν ἀσφαλέστερον ἡμῖν πορεύεσθαι 3. 2. 36.
Perhaps therefore it is safer for us to proceed.

Οὐκοῦν τῶν ἱππέων πολὺ ἡμεῖς ἐπ' ἀσφαλεστέρου ὀχήματός ἐσμεν 3. 2. 19.
Therefore we are on a far safer carrier than the horsemen.

Ὁρᾶτε δή 6. 5. 16. Ἔτι τοίνυν τάδε ὁρᾶτε 5. 1. 10.
Now consider. Therefore consider this also.

SUBORDINATING CONJUNCTIONS

368. Classification. — The subordinating conjunctions join dependent clauses to principal clauses, and many of them have become associated with a particular syntax in the clause governed. They may be classified as **declarative, causal, final, conditional, temporal, consecutive, modal,** and **local**.

369. Declarative Conjunctions. — The declarative conjunctions, governing substantive clauses, are ὅτι, *that;* ὡς, ὅπως, *how that, that* (cf. 297 ff.).

Δῆλον ὅτι πορεύεσθαι ἡμᾶς δεῖ 3. 2. 34.
It is plain that we must proceed.

Ἀνέκραγον ὡς οὐ δέοι ὁδοιπορεῖν 5. 1. 14.
They cried out that there was no need to journey by road.

Βουλεύεται ὅπως μήποτε ἔτι ἔσται ἐπὶ τῷ ἀδελφῷ 1. 1. 4.
He plans that he may never again be in his brother's power.

370. Causal Conjunctions. — The causal conjunctions are ὅτι, διότι, *because;* ἐπεί, ἐπειδή, *since* (cf. 200, 237).

Αὐτῷ ἐχαλεπάνθη ὅτι οὐκ εἰς κώμας ἤγαγεν 4. 6. 2.
He got angry with him because he did not lead them to any villages.

Ἐφ' ἁμάξης πορευόμενος διότι ἐτέτρωτο 2. 2. 14.
Proceeding on a wagon because he had been wounded.

Ἐπεὶ ὑμεῖς ἐμοὶ οὐκ ἐθέλετε πείθεσθαι 1. 3. 6.
Since you are not willing to obey me.

Χειρίσοφος μὲν ἡγοῖτο, ἐπειδὴ καὶ Λακεδαιμόνιός ἐστι 3. 2. 37.
Let Chirisophus lead, since he is a Lacedaemonian.

371. Final Conjunctions. — The final conjunctions are ἵνα, ὡς, ὅπως (ὄφρα, poet.), *that, in order that;* μή, *lest* (204, 205, 217, 229).

Ἵνα καὶ τὸ πλῆθος εἰδῶμεν 5. 1. 8.
That we may also know the number.

Ὡς μὴ πληγὰς λάβωμεν 4. 6. 16.
That we may not get a beating.

Τὰς ναῦς μετεπέμψατο, ὅπως ὁπλίτας ἀποβιβάσειεν 1. 4. 5.
He sent for the ships, that he might disembark hoplites.

Καί μοι τοῦτ' ἀγόρευσον ἐτήτυμον, ὄφρα εὖ εἰδῶ α 174.
And tell me this truly, that I may know it well.

Δεδιὼς μὴ λαβών με δίκην ἐπιθῇ 1. 3. 10.
Fearing lest he may arrest and punish me.

372. Conditional Conjunctions. — The conditional conjunctions, introducing conditional and concessive clauses, are εἰ (ἐάν, ἤν, ἄν), *if;* εἰ καί, *although*, καὶ εἰ, *even if* (203, 220, 232).

Οὐκ ἔστι τὰ ἐπιτήδεια, εἰ μὴ ληψόμεθα τὸ χωρίον 4. 7. 3.
There are no provisions unless we shall capture the place.

Εἰ καὶ οἴει με ἀδικοῦντά τι ἄγεσθαι, οὔτε ἔπαιον οὐδένα οὔτε ἔβαλλον
6. 6. 27.
Although you think that I am under arrest for a misdeed, I neither beat nor struck any one.

Ὁδοποιήσειέ γ' ἂν αὐτοῖς, καὶ εἰ σὺν τεθρίπποις βούλοιντο ἀπιέναι 3. 2. 24.
He would make a road for them, even if they should wish to depart with four-horse chariots.

373. Temporal Conjunctions. — The temporal conjunctions are ἐπεί, ἐπειδή, ὅτε, ὁπότε, ἡνίκα, ὡς, *when;* ἕως, ἔστε, ἄχρι, μέχρι, *until, as long as;* πρίν, *before, ere, until* (199, 222, 234, 251).

Ὅτ' ἀπῄει 5. 3. 6.
When he departed.

Ὁπότ' αὖ ἔγνως τὴν σαυτοῦ δύναμιν 1. 6. 7.
When again you came to recognize your own power.

Ἡνίκα δὲ τὸν πέμπτον (σταθμὸν) ἐπορεύοντο 3. 4. 24.
And when they were marching the fifth stage.

Ὡς ἤρξαντο θεῖν 4. 8. 19.
When they began to run.

Ἔως ἐπὶ τὰ Κόλχων ὅρια κατέστησαν τοὺς Ἕλληνας 4. 8. 8.
Until they brought the Greeks to the Colchian frontier.

Περιμένετε ἔστ' ἂν ἐγὼ ἔλθω 5. 1. 4.   Μέχρι σκότος ἐγένετο 4. 2. 4.
Wait till I come.   Till it grew dark.

Περιμένειν ἄχρι ἂν σχολάσῃ 2. 3. 2.   Πρὶν ἡ γυνὴ αὐτὸν ἔπεισε 1. 2. 26.
To wait till he finds leisure.   Until his wife persuaded him.

374. Consecutive Conjunctions. — The consecutive conjunctions, introducing result clauses, are ὥστε, ὡς, *so that, so as* (cf. 202, 252).

Ὁμίχλη ἐγένετο ὥστ' ἔλαθον 4. 2. 7.
A mist arose so that they escaped notice.

375. Modal and Local Connectives. — Modal and local clauses are introduced by relative adverbs of manner and place: such are ὡς, *as;* οὗ, ὅπου, *where;* ὅθεν, ὁπόθεν, *whence.*